CANON AND PROCLAMATION

CANON AND PROCLAMATION

Sermons for Our Times

Paul C. McGlasson

WILLIAM B. EERDMANS PUBLISHING COMPANY
GRAND RAPIDS, MICHIGAN / CAMBRIDGE, U.K.

Wm. B. Eerdmans Publishing Co.
255 Jefferson Ave. S.E., Grand Rapids, Michigan 49503 /
P.O. Box 163, Cambridge CB3 9PU U.K.

Printed in the United States of America

05 04 03 02 01 00   7 6 5 4 3 2 1

Library of Congress Cataloging-in-Publication Data

McGlasson, Paul.
Canon and proclamation: sermons for our times / Paul C. McGlasson.
p.   cm.
ISBN 0-8028-4731-5 (pbk.: alk. paper)
1. Bible — Sermons. 2. Sermons, English.   I. Title.

BS491.5.M37 2000
252′.051 — dc21
00-041728

www.eerdmans.com

To Peggy:
Life-partner in the joy of faith

CONTENTS

CONTENTS

Contents

FOREWORD

The importance of the sermon for the life of the church can hardly be overestimated. It remains a crucial test by which to measure Christian health and vitality. From the very inception of the church its greatest leaders have been, above all, preachers: Augustine, Chrysostom, Bernard, Luther, Calvin, Wesley, Newman, Spurgeon.

In spite of the many collections of sermons that fill our bookshops, the task of Christian proclamation has never been more difficult and taxing. The reasons for its demanding nature are also clear. First, the Christian preacher must be completely immersed in the full range of the biblical witness, equipped to probe deeply into its message with learning and imagination. Second, an effective sermon calls for lucid structure and theological shaping by which each individual pericope is given a sharp cutting edge in order to sound a powerful and coherent testimony to the gospel. Third, a sermon must address the Word of God to a flesh-and-blood congregation struggling to be faithful to both church and society in today's world.

One of the greatest legacies of the Reformation was its emphasis on the expository biblical sermon as the most suitable form by which to instruct its hearers in the language of faith. Its exposition sought to pursue the biblical sequence as a rule of faith in treating large blocks of material from both the Old and New Testaments. For various reasons in recent years the expository sermon has become virtually a lost art. Certainly the growth of biblical illiteracy among both clergy and laity has contributed to its erosion. It is also sad to note that misuse of the lectionary has often allowed slothful ministers to preach week after week only from the New Testament lessons. Probably the most distressing effect of modernity has been the widespread practice of flooding the sermon with a stream of anecdotes, which often amuse, but fail utterly to reckon with the role of the Holy Spirit, who opens up the biblical text to reveal its genuine relevance as a divine message offering repentance and rebirth.

In the light of this challenge to recover genuine expository preaching, it is a privilege to commend this collection of sermons by Paul McGlasson. It is indeed rare to find a scholar so deeply trained in the academic study of theology turn his full attention to the pastoral ministry along with all the duties it entails. He has recognized as few others in his generation that the front line in the battle for the soul of the modern church does not lie in the sophisticated debates of the university or in the endless church conferences on new strategies, but rather in the faithful proclamation of the Word in a small corner of God's vineyard.

These sermons arose from years of unrelenting work in a local parish and mark McGlasson's effort to chart a fresh beginning of expository preaching that will nurture the soil in preparation for divine renewal and rebirth. His sermons stand in close continuity with the great preachers of the past in requiring much from the hearer. These sermons are not given to entertain or to flaunt learning, but to probe deeply into the Bible, letting the inspired text sound to each hearer the needed Word from God. Above all, these sermons do not focus on the personality of the speaker, but point only to the living Lord of the church, who continues to wrestle with his people in new and unexpected ways.

BREVARD S. CHILDS
Sterling Professor of Divinity, Emeritus
Yale Divinity School

PREFACE

The sermons included in this volume were all delivered at Central Presbyterian Church in Stamford, Texas. Stamford is a small, rural community in the heart of west Texas. Though the economy is varied, it is largely based upon agriculture in the form of cotton farming. The farming is dry-land; water is scarce, and so there are no viable means of irrigation. When the rains come, the crops flourish, and the whole region is given an economic boost. When drought sets in, the crops all but disappear, and the resulting strain is felt by everyone. Stamford is blessed with an excellent school system, which often reaches the highest state levels of competition in both academics and athletics. Trees are scarce here, except for the ever-present mesquite; but the incredible beauty of the open range under the red glow of the evening sun more than compensates for the lack of extensive flora. The night sky is brilliant beyond comparison, for city lights are few and far between in this part of the country. The air is fresh, country air; and the weather changes before anyone knows what is going to happen.

The congregation has been in existence since 1899, a year before the founding of Stamford itself. Many of the present members are children, grandchildren, even great-grandchildren of founding families in the church. Every year a memorial service is held in which names of the deceased are read, followed by the tolling of the church bell. A rigid schedule of the church year is not followed; but the basic rhythms of the Christian calendar are closely observed and form the basis for celebration in the life of the community of faith. No effort has been made to eliminate the traces of local specificity in the sermons included here. I am profoundly grateful for the opportunity to have ministered in this splendid setting.

I would like to express my heartfelt thanks to the editor, Jennifer Hoffman, for her excellent advice. This volume is affectionately dedicated to my wonderful wife Peggy, whose contribution in every respect is completely immeasurable. Words cannot express the depth of my admiration for her wisdom, kindness, courage, and passionate love for life.

INTRODUCTION

The purpose of this volume can be very simply stated: it is an initial attempt to explore the question of Christian proclamation in the light of Brevard S. Childs's work on canon. On the one hand, the question is hardly new; every good sermon in the grand tradition of Christian witness has been based upon the reality of Scripture as canon, whether phrased in the form of *regula fidei, regula veritatis, sola Scriptura,* or the like. Yet, on the other hand, the question has never before even been raised, let alone closely examined. The reason for the need for a new appraisal is grounded in the substance of theology itself, for every new generation must come to grips with the subject matter of Scripture in a fresh way, and in our own age Childs's work on canon has revolutionized the study of the Bible. The study of each Testament in particular has been radically reoriented; the discipline of biblical theology has been revitalized with overwhelming force; genuine links with the heritage of the church have been carefully forged; and the prospects for exegesis are being explosively reconsidered. But the burning question of preaching is ripe for fresh study and reflection. Childs has powerfully argued that canon means proclamation; so then, given the reality of canon, how do we preach? The present volume of sermons, and the present introductory essay, are a first attempt to tackle this inviting issue; my hope is that it will contribute in some small way to a renaissance of Christian proclamation in the universal church.

The experience of constructing and delivering sermons as an ex-

1

periment in the relation of canon and proclamation has taught me two lessons. The first is that preaching itself is forever changed in the light of canon. There is no going back to models in the past, however extraordinary the examples of Christian preaching one might find. Nor is there any real comparison with the competing models of the present, whether conservative or liberal. Evangelical preaching, just as much as liberal preaching, is woefully ignorant of the reality of canon, and there are no bridges to be built here. Just as the gospel itself is *sui generis,* so also is the collection of Scripture that bears witness to it, and so too is the proclamation that takes place upon the basis of it; all else must fall to the wayside, forgotten. What that means practically is a supreme summons to hard work on the part of the pastor, who must not allow easy substitutes to distract from the task of genuine proclamation. And the second lesson is that canon brings with it a new conception of the theology of preaching. Here the links with the past are more observable, for the basic Reformation view of the *viva vox evangelii* is identical to the canonical conception of true preaching. Nevertheless, even here, a simple retreat is not possible, and a fresh attempt to articulate the theology of preaching is therefore mandated by the new discovery of canon in our time.

I

What are the elements of authentic proclamation from the perspective of canon? We begin with a great challenge: the exclusive entry-point into the canon of Scripture for contemporary proclamation is through the Hebrew and Greek text of the Christian Bible. That is to say, every sermon should be based upon careful study of the text in the original language by the pastor. I realize full well that this is to set a high standard; and yet, who does not agree that the standard is grounded in the very nature of the case? And if standards are not to be set here, where in human life ought they ever to be set? The fact is, there is simply no excuse for such a standard not to be universally observed in all Christian preaching henceforth. Regardless of conditions that may have obtained in the past, in our time resources are widely available for the study of Hebrew and Greek; good grammars abound, new lexical aids are published yearly, excellent teachers of both languages are resident in virtually every center of theological education that exists. Moreover, the convenient compromise, well-established in some circles, of promoting the understanding of Greek, but down-playing or even ignoring the study of Hebrew, is completely unacceptable from the point of view of canon. We have a collection of sacred Scriptures with two Testaments, each of which is to be heard in its unique voice, as well as together; canon therefore requires absolutely, without exception, that every sermon be based upon a firm grasp of the original text.

That this is not a rigid rule but a necessary criterion of genuine proclamation is easily affirmed by all who undertake the endeavor. There are nuances of language and construction in the original texts of both Testaments that defy every attempt to translate them; contrariwise, there are unintended nuances in English translations that are simply not present in the original language. Every pastor must be fully equipped to discern the subtleties of the text by firsthand reading of it. Commentaries, however complete and valuable a stimulus, are no substitute; expanded translations with notes, however well-meaning, are completely inadequate; the only way in which pastors can stand up on Sunday morning having done their best to preach a sermon based upon canon is to have prepared it from the Hebrew and Greek original. There is no other way.

Every individual passage of the Bible is located within a book; and every book is located within a part of the canon, such as Law, prophets, Gospels, Epistles, etc. Childs's work on canon has made very clear that every part of the Scriptures, as well as each book within the collection, is shaped to be preached.[1] Preaching is not the only use of the Bible; there is certainly a liturgical use, a private devotional use, and so forth. However, from the point of view of canon, the primary purpose of the shaping of Scripture is for the guidance of each new age of proclamation. The weekly work of sermon preparation therefore does not begin with "the problem of exegesis," or with "hermeneutical distance," or the like, which are false creations resulting from the misapplication of

---

1. See the two brilliant introductions by Childs: *Introduction to the Old Testament as Scripture* (Philadelphia: Fortress Press, 1979); and *The New Testament as Canon: An Introduction* (London: SCM Press, 1984). Regular consultation of these magnificent volumes is always a decisive stimulus in sermon preparation.

modern techniques of biblical study to the Bible. Instead, such work begins with the recognition that the text to be explored was shaped precisely for the purpose for which it is now about to be used. Canon is by definition an open invitation to proclamation, which always involves careful study of the canonical context of the passage of Scripture to be preached.

But a crucial point must be observed: the canonical shape of Scripture is identical to its final form. Modern study of the Bible has certainly uncovered historical layering, both in oral and written stages; and yet the ancient church did not hand on the stages of biblical growth, but only the Bible itself. The authority for Christian preaching is located in the final form of the text, not in a speculative attempt to dig behind it. Several issues are involved. The first point is that the pastor is not an outside critic of the church, but a teacher and scholar within the church. All Christian preaching begins by accepting the wisdom of the church concerning its own Scripture: that in the final form alone the truth can be found, not by clever attempts to reconstruct a different Bible. The second point is that the final form ties the work of the pastor together with the daily life of the listener, who reads the same Christian Bible. There is something tragic, even outrageous, about the arrogance of Christian preaching based upon a reconstructed text different from the final form in common use throughout all ages and everywhere. Nothing is learned by the congregation about the true substance of the faith; the only point reinforced is that the pastor has an "expertise" that others do not, and that is a sheer abuse of the pastoral office. And the third, and perhaps most important, point is that the final form of the text contains the truth, while the reconstructed stages of modern biblical study do not. The pastor will look in vain elsewhere to find the true word of life; it is found only in the canonical text.

Canon is shaped to be preached; that very fact implies two dimensions to genuine preaching. There is first of all explication of the text. With the original language carefully considered, with the canonical shape firmly fixed in mind, the first task of preaching is to comment and reflect upon the text itself. If it is a narrative it should be retold with dramatic vigor; if a prophetic oracle, unfolded with sharp contrasts; if a wisdom saying, elaborated upon with measured calculation; if a parable, recounted with analogical imagination; if an epistle,

4

closely examined with dialectical counterpoint. The point is that there is not a single formula for proper explication, for the simple reason that Scripture itself is given to us in such profound variety. Canonical shaping does not mean that the individuality of texts in the Bible are suppressed; it insures rather that their individuality will be rightly used in the future to discern the divine will. But the specificity of the text is precisely the avenue to the will of God that the canon of Scripture offers to the modern church. Careful explication of discrete passages based upon their own inherent integrity is a necessary check against any effort to reduce the true substance of Scripture to the simplistic jargons and slogans of modern pious religiosity, left or right.

And yet, it is also necessary to guard against reading each text in isolation from the whole, which is an open door to idiosyncratic misuse of the Bible. Whole theologies, from dispensationalism to liberation theology, have been erroneously built on a surface reading of the text of the Bible without the depth dimension that canon insures. There is one canon, one word of God, for the church. Consequently, every text, despite its individuality, is a contribution to a grasp of the one eternal will of God made known through the witness of Scripture. That is why biblical theology must be mastered by the pastor,[2] as well as introduction to the Bible; for in every attempt of the pastor to explicate a text for the congregation, the whole substance of the Christian witness is at stake. False leads can be inadvertently introduced, which will lead the congregation astray. The pastor is responsible for measuring the explication of the text by the true content of which it speaks, and that responsibility is implied in the very oath that the pastor takes in the ordination to the sacred office.

Explication means discovery, both for the pastor and for the congregation. Good preaching will often handle texts that have been learned by heart since childhood and that are deeply familiar to every

---

2. The magnum opus of theology since the Reformation is Childs's *Biblical Theology of the Old and New Testaments: Theological Reflection on the Christian Bible* (London: SCM Press, 1992). I am very concerned about the extent to which biblical theology is downplayed in theological education today, or considered as nothing more than a helping discipline to systematics. Biblical theology is the exercise of the primary teaching office of the church, and it should play a much greater role in theological education.

listener. And yet it will present those texts as if they are being heard for the first time, in wide-eyed wonder. The fact is, there is always something new to see in the Bible that was never noticed before, and that somehow renders the entire message in a completely new light. This is where the hard work of sermon preparation pays off. Careful study of the original languages, close analysis of the canonical shape of the text, as full a grasp of biblical theology as one can attain — if used well, such efforts will invariably yield fresh insight, often startling realization. The key to investigation is the basic approach of the pastor, which can only be one of eager anticipation of the new reality that every text of the Bible mirrors. The beauty of truth yields itself only to the joy of sheer adoration. In the end, Scripture itself deserves nothing less, for rapt attention to the language of faith is only fitting given the subject matter of which it speaks.

The second dimension of Christian proclamation based upon canon is application. The essential point, which I must make at once, is that application is not somehow a foreign substance added to biblical study from "spirituality" or "piety"; application, on the contrary, is mandated by the reality of canon itself. The whole point of canon is to render the message of the apostles and the prophets in such a way as to guide the future life of the community of faith. It is the pastor's duty, therefore, to provide that guidance upon the basis of Scripture. The explication of the text is the necessary foundation both for the pastor's own work and for the actual structure of the sermon. Yet application is not a wooden attempt to "update" the biblical message; it is necessarily to lay before the congregation the absolute claim of the gospel upon their whole existence in every aspect of human living. Needless to say, this dimension of preaching is just as taxing of the abilities of the pastor as explication and requires the same degree of effort. But where is the effort to be placed?

A negative comment is in order first. By far the standard approach at this point on both the left and the right is to summon up various forms of "illustrations" to fill in the needed application. Such illustrations come ready-prepared in various sermon "helps" or are derived from occasional reading in newspapers, magazines, etc. They may be well intended to perform this side of proclamation. However, illustrations are completely null and void as far as preaching from the canon of Scripture is concerned. Illustrations are a symptom of the terrible decay of modern preaching and of the need for wholesale reform at the very roots. They may be good entertainment, but they are not good preaching; indeed, good preaching on the basis of canon should contain no illustrations whatsoever. I shall press my point a step further, even at the risk of giving offense to some. Illustrations in sermons are a sign of the laziness and distractibility of the modern pastorate when it comes to the crucial task of visitation. Modern pastors who are not engaged in regular visitation of their members have lost touch with the everyday life of Christian people. Thus they fill their sermons with useless illustrations rather than the precious reality of the everyday life of faith. If regular visitation were routinely practiced by every pastor, however time-consuming that task may be, there would never again be another "illustration" in a Christian sermon.

But in the end the positive formulation far overshadows the negative. Modern Christians come to church expecting, hoping for, desiring practical guidance in the daily walk of faith. They come with such an attitude because Scripture itself demands just such a concern to be paramount for the call of discipleship. The obligation of pastors is to meet this need to the very best of their ability. A programmatic system here is not in order. One cannot somehow manufacture good sermonic application using a set amount of chosen ingredients. A pastor should be fully engaged in regular visitation and pastoral care of the needy and vulnerable; a pastor should be pursuing personal growth in the forms of human culture in all its variety; a pastor should be an intelligent observer of national and world events. All of these resources, deployed in whatever way seems best in the given moment, should be used in every paragraph of application. Endless creativity is to be kept in motion, for the community of faith is a living organism with changing needs, and a timely and responsive address of those needs is a pastoral requirement.

A final comment is in order about the elements of preaching from a canonical perspective. We have spoken of explication and application, and the ways in which canon provides for both. But another dimension of Christian proclamation hovers over the sermon as a whole, whether it appears as a specific part or not: and that is the force of challenge to the congregation. Sermons are not a performance, despite the sideshow atmosphere of much televangelism. They should never, under any circumstances, dribble off into the trivial or be interlaced with pleasant fluff. The issues being preached about are matters of life and death. There is nothing more important to all human existence than to hear the Word of God and respond appropriately. It is up to the pastor to preach in such a way as to make that point clear. If sermons lack serious purpose, they will receive polite approval — and be completely ignored. If sermons strike at the heart of the matter, not just once but again and again, and never let go until full justice is done to the majesty of God's will, then they will be heeded.

II

The Reformation doctrine of Christian preaching can be encapsulated in a single formula: the preaching of the Word of God is the Word of God. Our task here is to reaffirm this view, and yet to do so in the light of a fresh understanding of the nature of Scripture itself.

The profound existential immediacy of the biblical message in all parts of the Christian canon has not been submerged by the final shaping, but retained. Whether in the form of Pauline parenesis, or the direct address of the Old Testament prophets, or the explicit circumstances of the struggling psalmist, or the trials and tribulations of apocalyptic writings, the specificity is everywhere retained. Yet, on the other hand, the collection of sacred Scriptures has been received and handed on to the church as the one eternal will of God for all times and in all places. There is no other source for the knowledge of God. How is one to grasp at the same time the universal claim of Scripture as a whole and the detailed circumstantiality of its witness? To treat Scripture as a time-conditioned voice from antiquity is to deny the faith of the church since its inception, which has always held that the authority of Scripture is supreme and self-validating. Yet to ignore the inherent vitality of the biblical witness in all its variety of detail is to render its voice mute at best, heretical at worst. The only perspective from which to grasp the true paradox contained in the very form of the Bible is the theology of Christian proclamation.

To begin with, the canonical conception of preaching is radically christological. The authority of Scripture is grounded in the present rule of Christ, the one Head of the church. The rule of Christ extends to all creation; nothing hinders his glorious purpose, and nothing restricts the accomplishment of his sovereign will. Yet where is his voice heard in the church today? What is the point of contact between the glory of the risen Lord and the listening world? The answer is the weekly sermon. However shaky the voice of the preacher may be, however fearful the one who sends it forth, however overwhelming the challenge that it represents, the voice of Christian preaching is the voice of Christ. To ignore it is to ignore him; to obey it is to obey him; to do it to the best of one's ability is to serve Christ in the role of pastor of the flock of God. There is no other goal or agenda for Christian preaching: it is not there for the purpose of entertainment, or to stir up trouble, or to solve the world's problems. To preach rightly is to preach Jesus Christ, the one hope of the whole earth.

The energy of Christian preaching is the presence of God's Spirit, and not human capacity in any manifestation. Preaching is not the liberating projection of human imagination, nor the systematic deduction of human reason, nor the expression of exalted human spirituality. The source of all truth, the origin of all illumination, is the Spirit of God. Preaching is an office of the church, and as with every other office is endowed with the gifts of the Spirit. The presence of God's Spirit guides the pastor from the text of Scripture to the substance of proclamation, renders the word of preaching the very word of God to a specific local church in the particular situation of its common life, and opens the minds and hearts of the listeners to the true appreciation of what is preached. That is why the chief act of sermon preparation is to call upon the guidance of the Spirit; that is why the order of service includes a prayer for illumination just prior to the preaching of the word. The promise of God's Spirit is the future of all Christian preaching, and in the end to ask for the Spirit's guidance is the true invitation to reformation of the church.

But what, then, is preached? If it is not political advice, or human piety, or entertaining trivia, or a propositional system, then what? The subject matter of Christian preaching is the truth. As Christians, we believe that Scripture is the one measure of all truth in creation. Scripture is the mirror in which the glory of God in his universe is perfectly reflected. Preaching upon the basis of canon is not an exercise in personal development, nor a platform for fine opinions, however clever. Preaching is the herald of truth for all the earth. It will not give in to party pressure, no matter how great the promise of reward; it will not lose its self-confidence, no matter how desperate the resistance; it will not falter, no matter how alluring the distractions. For all time, and for all the earth, the role of Christian proclamation is to bear witness to the truth to all humanity. There could not be a more serious endeavor; there could not be a greater responsibility; there could not be a deeper joy.

Finally, the aim of preaching upon the basis of canon is transformation of everyday existence in obedience to the command of Christ. Proclamation and discipleship go hand in hand: the former must always lead to the latter, while the latter is not possible without the former. That is the reason for the firm insistence upon the practicality of application; for genuine preaching is not an escape from reality — into the past or into the future — but a total alteration of it. The whole human person is engaged by the preaching of the word: the mind, in its earnest attempt to see the fullness of God's being in his infinite marvel; the will, in its endeavor to close off all avenues of evasion and make the right choice leading to new life; the emotions, in the freedom of passionate embrace of the gifts of God in the miracle of his universe; the body, in the acknowledgment of the treasures of life contained within the limits of the divine order. Conformity to Christ with one's whole being: that is the goal of the word of God rightly preached, and rightly heard.

I

FROM THE LIFE OF JACOB

1. Genesis 25:19-34

Today we begin a series of sermons based on the Old Testament patriarch Jacob. The biblical account of the life of Jacob is contained in the middle chapters of the book of Genesis. Like his father Isaac and his grandfather Abraham, Jacob is the special recipient of the divine promise of land and a people. The Old Testament speaks of God's promise to Abraham, Isaac, and Jacob, a promise by which Israel lived and to which it looked forward in hope. But of the three patriarchs, Jacob stands out as the one who undergoes the most intense personal struggle. At times he is somewhat reluctant; at other times he is extremely aggressive. But at all times he is met by a God who will not let go of his eternal purpose in Jacob's life. Let us consider over these next few weeks the challenge that Jacob poses for our understanding of the Christian life. Brothers and sisters, hear the Word of God.

Isaac, the son of Abraham, marries Rebekah. Isaac is forty years old when they are married. Rebekah remains childless for twenty years after their marriage; but then one day Isaac prays to God for a child, and Rebekah conceives. It turns out that she is pregnant with twins. Unfortunately, it is a difficult pregnancy; the text states vividly that the two children crush one another in her womb. She turns to God in despair, seeking to understand the meaning of her suffering. The answer she receives from God is startling. He tells her that her two children are destined to become the founders of two different peoples, grouped into two different nations. And furthermore, as if to compound the mystery, one of the two nations will be subject to the other one. And even more amazing, against every custom of the time, the older child shall be subject to the younger child.

We begin our reflections upon the story of Jacob with a question: When did God set his seal of love upon you? When did God choose you to be his servant? When did God adopt you as his very own? Perhaps some would answer that it was when you became a Christian, or when you joined the church, or when you were baptized. But the witness of Scripture points in a very different direction. God chose you before you ever took a single breath. In fact, God chose you before he made a world independent of himself. Even then, before a world existed, he already knew your name; even then, he already determined to bring manifold blessing into your life; even then, he already planned to use you in his service in the world. Before he made creation, you were not only known to God; you were loved by him, embraced by him, cared for by him, cherished by him. It was not because of any special qualities that you possess; rather, it was simply because of God's desire to love you as his own.

The difficult pregnancy is finally over. Rebekah gives birth to her twin sons. From the moment of their birth, they are as different as night and day. The first, whom they name Esau, is born full of color. The second, named Jacob, is born grasping on to Esau's heal. Jacob's eagerness is clearly a sign of what is to come. The different boys grow up into two very different men. Esau is an outdoorsman, who loves to hunt and bring home game for his father to eat. He is at home in the open country. Jacob, on the other hand, stays pretty much close to home. The Hebrew word that describes him is ambiguous: it can mean either morally innocent or simply "ordinary." But the connotation is clear: Jacob doesn't get into trouble. Esau is the favorite of his father Isaac, who loves to eat what he brings home and cooks. Jacob, on the other hand, is the favorite of his mother Rebekah.

The call to discipleship does not remain within the narrow limits of our experience of the world. On the contrary, it challenges those limits, expands them, and stretches them, at times seemingly close to their breaking point. Jacob is a young man accustomed to a quiet life at

12

home; and yet he is now within inches of entering into the adventure of a lifetime. Everything that he has counted on for his entire life is about to be taken from him: his family, his home, his possessions. In a short while, he will be fleeing from his homeland to a foreign land and will face a whole series of challenges to overcome. Soon Jacob, a born homebody, will be living in the open countryside, where he will meet God face-to-face. God's electing love does not guarantee an untroubled existence free of worry and stress. Indeed, there are times when it seems that the very opposite is true. Those whom God elects as his own he purposefully brings through difficult trials, and puts into new situations, and confronts with fresh obstacles — not in order to defeat or crush us, but because he wants from us the very best that we have to offer, and he will not be satisfied with less. The same God who challenges us also gives us more resources than we could ever have possibly expected.

The text has set the background in the early life of Jacob and Esau. It has rendered a telling description of the differences in their personalities and interests. Now it slows down to focus upon one incident, which sets events in motion for years to come. Jacob is cooking a pot of lentil soup. Esau returns from the countryside, completely exhausted from physical exertion and hunger. Esau begs Jacob to give him some of the red stuff he's cooking; he is famished. But Jacob has a trick up his sleeve. He sees Esau's desperate condition, and so he offers a deal. He will feed Esau, if Esau will relinquish to him the rights of the first-born child. Esau quickly calculates the pluses and minuses of the proposed exchange and concludes that he has nothing to lose — what good is a birthright to a dead man? So he accepts. But Jacob won't relent; he forces Esau to take an oath. And Esau swears his birthright over to Jacob. Jacob quickly offers the food to Esau. The Hebrew text piles up four verbs in quick succession: Esau ate, he drank, he rose up, he left. The dramatic sequence describes what appears on the surface to be a routine daily event. And then it underscores the horror of what he has done: Esau has shown utter contempt for his own birthright. The passage makes no comment on the way in which Jacob acquired the birthright. Clearly, though, his gaining of the birthright overturns completely the established custom.

The real struggle of the Christian life takes place in the practical experience of everyday life. It is in the way we relate to our family, our friends, and our co-workers and in the way we carry out our duties in life that Christian discipleship is shaped and refined. It is all too easy to push aside daily routine as inconsequential to the reality of God's kingdom. But Scripture moves in the opposite direction. Daily life is where the crucial decisions of faith are in fact made. Esau is a critical example of a decision wrongly made. Esau's error is to assume that mundane matters such as food and drink have no relevance to the divine blessing. But in fact Scripture makes clear that genuine growth in discipleship occurs most clearly in the ordinary matters of human existence. We are reminded by Esau not to overlook the eternal significance of routine living.

We are also instructed in a more positive way by the example of Jacob. Even here, there is a certain ambiguity. Jacob clearly plays on Esau's weakness in order to get what he wants. Scripture withholds judgment on Jacob's tactics, but they are certainly less than generous. What Jacob does rightly exemplify is the true single-mindedness of Christian discipleship. We live in a world filled with "opportunity." From every direction we are given offers that will "change our lives forever." New products will enhance our welfare; new ideas will revolutionize our thinking; new dreams will guarantee our future. Now, there are indeed exciting opportunities in the time in which we live, perhaps more so than at any other time in human history. The Christian is wise to seize good opportunities that come along, with the promise of fruits for the service of Christ. But how will you know? How will you know when to give an eager yes, or when to give a polite but firm no? In the final analysis, the true measure is that given by Christ himself. Does it promote the love of God above everything else, and love of neighbor as yourself? Then go for it; give it all you've got. On the other hand, does it call either of these into question, in even the slightest degree? Then just walk away.

2. Genesis 27

We continue today our series of sermons based on the story of Jacob. Last week we recounted the birth of Jacob, born already trying to seize

14

the birthright from his twin brother Esau. We observed the differences between the two young men and the total change of life that Jacob is about to undergo. We heard of Jacob's wily effort to trick Esau out of his birthright and noticed Esau's foolish willingness to let go of permanent blessing for the sake of short-term, temporary gain. In our reflections, we began to consider the illumination that the figure of Jacob brings to Christian living, and especially the astonishing new experiences to which the call of discipleship brings us. The activity of God in our lives is not limited to previous experience; instead, it opens the door to fresh encounter with his living person. Today let us focus upon yet another occasion in which Jacob wrests away the blessing from his brother Esau. Brothers and sisters, hear the Word of God.

Isaac is now very old, and it is time to carry out the custom of passing along the blessing of inheritance to a new generation. He calls his firstborn son, Esau, and tells him to prepare a tasty meal of fresh game, in preparation for receiving his inherited rights. But Rebekah, Isaac's wife, overhears the conversation and quickly takes matters into her own hands. She immediately informs her son Jacob what has occurred and gives him a detailed plan of action. Jacob is to bring two goats from the flock — there is no time to go on an actual hunt, for they must beat Esau to the punch — which Rebekah will use to cook the meal she knows her husband enjoys. The skin of the animals will also be used as part of the elaborate deception by which Jacob will gain the blessing from his father Isaac. Meanwhile, Rebekah finds one of Esau's best garments for Jacob to wear. It is a daring and brilliant plan, anticipating every eventual move of Isaac. At first, Jacob is reluctant, in strange contrast to his earlier aggressive behavior. He fears he will be found out and dismissed as a fraud. He does not understand his mother's ingenuity, so she simply tells him that she will accept upon herself any negative consequences of his actions. But at all costs he must act, and act quickly; there is no time to lose.

There are plenty of issues in life that call for flexibility, open-mindedness, and adaptability. When we face such issues, the wiser course is to keep all our options open and to probe and search until the best alternative presents itself. But there are other circumstances in which a very different approach is required. We will all at times face crucial issues in life where decisive action is called for. Here, the only legitimate option is to do what needs to be done, to forget the past, and to move on in life. It doesn't matter what anyone else thinks or says; what matters is that we stick to our decision and never look back. Such decisions always involve a certain amount of risk, and that risk cannot be removed. God sometimes puts us in positions where we have to take a chance in life or lose the promise of his blessing. But what we will always discover is that what lies on the other side of that risk is more abundance than we ever dreamed.

Jacob carries out the plan of his mother Rebekah. He approaches his father Isaac, who is virtually blind. Isaac asks who has come to see him, and Jacob tells him that it is Esau, who has returned to carry out his father's wishes. Isaac is immediately suspicious: How has he returned so fast? Jacob deftly dodges one bullet: God provided the animal. But Isaac won't give in so easily, and he tells Jacob to come closer. Isaac touches Jacob, but thankfully the animal hair covers his exposed skin. A second bullet is dodged: "The voice is Jacob's voice, but the hands are the hands of Esau." Isaac eats the meal that has been prepared, but he continues to suspect a trap. So he has Jacob come close in order to kiss him. The scene is excruciatingly intense; one slip-up and Jacob is done for. He draws near, but once again Rebekah's genius has covered every base. Isaac smells Esau's clothes and proceeds to the blessing. He holds nothing back in the blessing, extending to Jacob the full promise of divine bounty in every dimension of life. He wishes him a full life of material plenty, a prominent place in human history and society, and divine protection from every enemy.

What can we expect when we take the risk of faith? We discover first of all that life is incomparably richer once the wager of faith has been laid down. What we may have lost is quickly seen to be as less than nothing compared to what we have gained. God may take away something valuable; but he replaces it with something priceless. God may remove us from the ease of security; but he places us in the incredible excitement of new challenges and unsuspected treasures. He may cut short well-made plans; but he replaces them with his own eternal design, whereby he teaches us to give every last ounce of effort that we have to give. If we refuse the risk of faith we may keep what we have, but we will never know what we have lost. But if we accept the risk of faith, we inherit more than we ever thought possible.

From the Life of Jacob

The scene remains the same, but a new character arrives who changes everything. Esau returns with food from the hunt, according to his father's request. Esau knows nothing of what has happened, and so he brings the meal to Isaac. Isaac can only ask: Who are you? And Esau tells him. The reaction of Isaac is intense and immediate: he is utterly devastated. He can only stammer in sudden realization of what has occurred: "Then who? who is the one that came, and I ate, and blessed him, and he is the one that will be blessed?" If Isaac's reaction is intense, Esau's is even more fierce. He is bitterly enraged when he realizes that he has been bested again by Jacob, and he pitifully begs his father for a blessing. But Isaac explains that the blessing has already been given to his brother Jacob, and it cannot be revoked. Esau furiously excoriates his brother, playing on his name Jacob, which means "the one who circumvents." Again he begs his father for a blessing, any blessing at all. But again Isaac explains that every possible blessing has already been given to his brother Jacob. Esau breaks down completely and appeals for some kind of blessing in utter despair. Isaac finally relents and promises Esau that he will one day break the hold of Jacob's rule.

The intense chapter concludes by recording the aftermath of the event. It states frankly that from now on Esau hates his brother Jacob and bears an overwhelming grudge. The only consolation Esau can find is to plot Jacob's murder, as soon as their father Isaac has passed away. Rebekah finds out about his twisted plans and once again encourages Jacob to take bold action. She tells him to leave the country and to flee to the faraway home of her brother Laban. But even the wise Rebekah miscalculates the timing; she believes that Esau's rage will simmer down in a short while, at which point Jacob can return. In fact, Jacob will not return for twenty years. Rebekah complains to Jacob that Esau's life — his choice of Hittite wives has plagued her and Isaac — has brought her nothing but grief. And so she sends Jacob off. But before he goes, in a beautiful and deeply moving postscript, Isaac calls Jacob back and repeats the blessing that he has already given him. In fact, he makes fully clear that the blessing given to Jacob is the very promise of land and posterity first given to his father Abraham. Jacob not only has everything; he has the greatest gift of all.

What will you do, brothers and sisters, when plans in life go awry?

I would suspect that you have all faced situations in which cherished hopes have been disappointed and special dreams have been unfulfilled. We cannot say that such disappointment is contrary to God's will, for we know full well that God does what he pleases and that no events are outside of his sovereign control. But the life of Jacob gives us a clue to the mystery of God's work in human life. From Jacob's point of view, all seems lost, and he is on the run for his very life. But from our point of view as readers of the story we see the amazing plan of God in the making. The woman Jacob will fall in love with and marry is not in Canaan; she is in a distant country. At home, Jacob would have had to contend with Esau for every scrap. But in the land where he is going, he is free to acquire enormous wealth of possessions. God does not take away what we want because he hates us. Rather, he does so because he has something far better in mind. He puts us in life exactly where we will flourish the most. We do not know what lies ahead; but we do know that it will be the very best that life has to offer. And the reason is because we know the Lord of life, who withholds nothing of joy and pleasure from the lives of his children.

3. Genesis 29:1-30

We continue today our series of sermons on the patriarch Jacob, whose struggles in life set him apart from the other patriarchs of Israel. Twice Jacob outwits his brother Esau. The first time results in the passing of the birthright from Esau to Jacob, while the second time brings about the blessing of Jacob instead of Esau by their father Isaac. But the second time, a price has to be paid; Jacob must go into exile in order to avoid the murderous rage of his brother. He sets out on a long journey to look for his future, now that his past has been taken away. Let us consider today the marvelous treasure that he finds at the end of the road. Brothers and sisters, hear the Word of God.

It is Rebekah, Jacob's mother, who first tells her son to flee. She tells him to return to her own homeland, in Haran, and to seek out her brother Laban. But then Isaac himself gives the same command to Jacob. Isaac charges Jacob to go to Haran to look for a wife from among the daughters of Laban. The reason is clearly stated: to avoid taking a wife from among the women of Canaan. So Jacob sets out eastward and arrives in Haran. He comes with nothing, except the promise of Almighty God pronounced upon him by his father Isaac. He arrives in the middle of a very ordinary scene in daily life. Several flocks of sheep are gathered around a well of water, but the well is sealed with a giant stone. The normal routine is described in the text: the local flocks are all gathered together at the well, at which point the stone is removed and the sheep are allowed to drink; then the huge stone is replaced. Jacob inquires of the people who are gathered: "Where are you from?" And they tell him they are from Haran. He then asks if they are acquainted with Laban, and they say they are. Jacob asks concerning Laban's welfare, and they reply that he is doing well, and that in fact his daughter Rachel is about to arrive with her flock. Now already, even before he meets them, Jacob has taken a personal interest in Laban and his family. He knows Rachel is coming with her flock, and that the stone is still covering the well; so he asks why it cannot be removed immediately. After all, there is still plenty of daylight left for grazing the flock. But they respond by describing the usual custom and let it go at that.

The figure of Jacob helps us to understand the growth of a new generation of faith. Nothing is more crucial for the church than the training in discipleship of each new age of its ongoing life. The one gospel by which each new generation lives is the same gospel by which the church has always lived in every circumstance of its life. The blessing of God is tied forever to the true proclamation of that one gospel. But it is also crucial to remember that each new age faces a fresh set of problems to solve. The insights of the past must be preserved; but they cannot simply be repeated, or they will lose their power to illuminate. Every new generation of Christians must seek to speak the language of faith anew in their own time and place and to wrestle with the questions and issues that arise. And in our own time, is not the primary concern of the Christian church the practice of faith in ordinary common life? Is not the cutting edge of the church's life the effort to discern the living will of God in the routines of everyday experience?

Jacob is still in the midst of his conversation with the people of Haran when Rachel herself walks up. She is the daughter of Laban and has the task of tending her family's flock. As soon as Jacob sees Rachel coming with her sheep, he removes the heavy stone from the well and proceeds to water her animals. Then he kisses Rachel and with a rush of emotion tells her that her father and his mother are brother and sister. When she finds out that he is Rebekah's son, she races off to tell Laban. Laban in turn comes quickly to see for himself, and he discovers that indeed his own sister's son has suddenly appeared from out of nowhere. Laban throws his arms around Jacob, and kisses him, and brings him to their home. He expresses his joy in their kinship, and a long relationship begins to unfold.

As Christians, we all share with the world a wide variety of institutions and customs. We are all grouped into families; we all participate in the economic structures that govern our material well-being; we all owe allegiance to the government that protects our rights. The Christian faith does not remove us from these institutions, and it condemns along with everyone else a fanaticism that would seek to destroy them. But here, another line of thought must also be added. For the Christian faith does breathe new life into the way we relate to others in all these dimensions of human existence. The structure of the family is not abolished; and yet the relationship of man and wife is transformed forever by the call of discipleship. Economic institutions are not overturned; and yet the Christian's basic direction in life is not determined by financial reward. The state is honored and its freedoms are cherished; and yet the Christian is not to be fooled by false promises that no human being can keep.

After a brief period of settling in, the relationship between Laban and Jacob begins to take a different turn. Jacob has been helping out, and so Laban offers compensation for his labors. He asks Jacob what he wants in return for his service, and Jacob leaves no doubt what his intentions are. Laban has two daughters, the older daughter Leah, who has some form of affliction of her eyes, and his younger daughter Rachel. Rachel is extremely attractive, and clearly Jacob is utterly taken with her. And so he tells Laban: I will give you seven years of service in return for Rachel's hand in marriage. Laban agrees; he somewhat indifferently describes the deal as a good one, since otherwise she would be given to someone outside the family. But for Jacob, the deal could hardly be better, for seven years is nothing in return for the love of his life.

20

The Christian life brings with it a whole new set of priorities, which completely defy rational calculation and logic. The measure of life is no longer in terms of the short-term gains that our decisions and actions might bring. The call to discipleship brings a certain depth to our lives, which puts every plan we make into a new perspective. There are some goals in life that are worth infinitely more than whatever losses we may suffer along the way in order to obtain them. The wise Christian will not think twice about those losses; rather, the focus is upon the extraordinary kindnesses of God that accompany our steps in each new stage of life. No Christian is immune from temptation to distractions, which would in fact draw us away from the reality of divine blessing. But the answer of the Christian is to ignore the distractions for the sake of the incredible wealth of goodness that God showers upon us.

Things could not possibly be going better for Jacob. The seven years have passed like a single instant, and so he requests that Laban carry out his end of the bargain. Laban consents and organizes a wedding celebration. However, Laban plays a cruel trick on Jacob. When the wedding night arrives and the bride is sent to the groom to consummate their marriage, he sends Leah instead of Rachel. The following morning Jacob realizes what has occurred and confronts Laban. Laban offers as a lame excuse the accepted custom of the marriage of the firstborn prior to the younger daughter. But clearly he is simply taking advantage of Jacob's generosity. Laban offers a modified version of their initial deal: Rachel's hand right away, if Jacob will serve another seven years. Jacob agrees, and though he now has two wives, his affection remains centered on Rachel. As the story unfolds in the chapters that follow, Jacob continues his service to Laban even beyond the time of their renewed bargain. In the end, Jacob recovers the initiative and turns the tables on Laban; he eventually acquires great wealth at Laban's expense. He finishes his twenty years in Haran with a large family, numerous servants, and huge flocks of animals.

Brothers and sisters, the blessing of God does not remove us from the suffering of disappointments and even severe trials. Such trials are not easy, and the Christian shares with the rest of the world the pain and suffering that life can bring. But here you must pause and ask: How will you react when you face such a trial? You cannot turn aside from the path in life that God has laid out before you. Sometimes the best you can do may be simply to carry on; but at all costs you must remain constant and eager in the duties of life that God has given to you. The paradox of grace is that even in the midst of suffering, God gives us astonishing gains that completely overshadow the losses. God may bring us through difficult circumstances in life; yet we discover that the purpose of the hardships has been to guide us to a whole new world of undiscovered insights, unheard of dreams, uncharted beauty, and incredible joys. Don't ever lose hope!

4. Genesis 32

We conclude today our series of sermons based on the life of the patriarch Jacob. We saw last week how Jacob was forced to flee to a foreign land, where he meets and marries his beautiful wife Rachel. Jacob came to Haran with nothing, but he has now acquired a wonderful family and numerous possessions. He is a happy and wealthy man. But God commands him to return to the land of Canaan, which is the land of promise for God's people. And one thing still stands in the way: the wrath of his brother Esau. Today let us consider how Jacob faces the final challenge and the light his actions shed upon the struggle of faith that we must all undergo throughout life. Brothers and sisters, hear the Word of God.

Jacob already knows the enormous obstacle he will encounter up ahead. Esau has taken up residence in the land of Edom, which is to the east and south of Canaan. Jacob is traveling west, and so his journey home puts him directly in the path of the brother who once planned his murder. Jacob sends an advance party to sound Esau out. They are to inform Esau of the blessings Jacob has received and to remind him of the long time he has remained away from home in deference to his brother. But they return to Jacob with the worst possible news: Esau is coming toward them and is bringing with him a huge band of men. Jacob is terrified; but he devises a clever plan on the spot to counter the threat posed by his brother. He divides his family and his possessions into two groups, to be sent along two divergent paths. If Esau's intentions are hostile, he reasons, at least this way a portion of his family and wealth will survive. What is at issue behind his actions is God's promise of a future for his people; Jacob will not give in, even when that promise is up against overwhelming odds.

The Christian life does not take place in a historical vacuum. Every age of the church has faced a new set of challenging circumstances. Everyone who follows the daily news can see the enormous danger that assaults the church from every side. On the theological right, we are threatened by an intolerant bigotry that would legislate Christian morality for the rest of the world. On the theological left, we are equally threatened by an easy compromise that would gladly sell out the gospel for the sake of mass appeal. Now, the proper response is not to ignore the threats, as if they do not exist. We can no more escape the times in which we live than we can jump over our own shadow. But neither can we let go, even for one instant, of the gracious promise of God to see his beloved church through every trial. Our only choice is to exercise all our imagination and skill in carrying out the tasks in life that God has given us, leaving to God alone the responsibility for accomplishing his promise.

Jacob turns to God in prayer in the midst of his trying ordeal. He addresses the God of his father Abraham, and the God of his father Isaac; he is fully aware that his ancestors are no strangers to difficult circumstances. Abraham was promised by God the whole land of Canaan, a promise that he believed in hope; and yet he died in possession of nothing but a small cave in which he buried his wife Sarah. Isaac was forced by famine to leave the promised land for the land of the Philistines, though he amassed a considerable fortune there. For all his troubles, Jacob is facing difficulties that God's people have always faced; and he turns to the one true God, upon whom they have always called. Jacob marvels at the incredible kindnesses that have been shown to him, though his life is so insignificant. He crossed the Jordan one way with nothing but his journeying stick; yet now he is about to cross back with not one but two hoards of treasure. He asks God for protection from the danger that Esau poses to his family. And he reminds God of the promise that he gave him, to multiply his posterity and to bring wonderful blessing into his life.

It is all too easy to conclude in the midst of trying circumstances that God has abandoned us. Why must we face such difficulties? Why must we go through such burdensome trials? But perhaps it is wise to be reminded occasionally that we are not alone in our suffering. We may face a new set of challenges; but we are by no means the first generation of Christians to be up against considerable odds. On the contrary, the brightest periods in the church's life are clearly matched with the lowest depths to which it has sunk. This paradox, however mysterious, is no accident. When easy success and certain triumph are taken from us, we suddenly remember the source of every blessing that we receive. It is not our own hands: we came naked from our mother's womb, and we will return naked to the earth. It is not our own efforts in life: the good life of divine blessing is not a reward for human merit. Rather, the source of blessing is God's eternal love, whereby he chose us even before there was ground to till or animals to keep. Even in trying circumstances, we should not neglect to thank God for his many blessings and to ask for his continued compassion.

Jacob tries one more tactic to pacify his brother Esau. He selects a large variety of animals to be given to his brother as a gift. It is an ingenious idea; each kind of animal is driven in a herd, to be presented to his brother Esau one herd at a time. Jacob instructs his servants to maintain a space between each of the herds. The idea is that Esau will be placated, not once, but several times in succeeding waves of generosity — all in the hope that the intensity of his anger toward his brother will be mitigated. He sends the flocks for Esau on ahead and stays behind with his family and possessions. But that night he packs up all that he has, gathers his family together, and sends them over the brook Jabbok, a tributary of the Jordan River. Once they have all crossed over, Jacob is left alone.

All of us here in this room are incredibly blessed by the small town in which we live. Here faces are recognized, names are known, joys are shared, and burdens are mutually carried. And we are also given astonishing riches in the wondrous fellowship that we share in this congregation, a true community that cannot be matched in so-called megachurches. But despite the joys and blessings of community, there is still a need for an individual response of faith. In the end, no one can say yes to Christ for us; that response must come from our own words and our own deeds.

All his family and wealth are on one side of the river, and Jacob is on the other. And there he encounters God in a most amazing way. Jacob wrestles with God's angel for an entire night. And perhaps even more startling, Jacob doesn't lose the fight. At one point in their match, the angel touches Jacob on the thigh and dislocates it; but still Jacob wrestles on. Finally, the angel asks to be released, for the dawn is about to arrive. But Jacob refuses to release him until the angel gives him a blessing. The angel asks for his name, and Jacob tells him; then the angel changes Jacob's name to Israel. The name Israel is related to the Hebrew word for prince, so the angel states that Jacob has indeed won — like a prince — in his struggle with both God and humankind. Jacob asks for the angel's name, but he refuses to give it; instead he gives him a blessing. Jacob realizes that he has been wrestling with God himself, and so he names the place accordingly. Finally, the dawn arrives, and Jacob limps off toward the promised land.

Brothers and sisters, we conclude our series of sermons on the figure of Jacob by being reminded of the role of the body in Christian discipleship. There is not a person here today who has not faced hardship in the form of bodily suffering. You all carry about with you physical marks by which Christ has stamped you as his own. Why does he do so? Why does he reach into your life with physical suffering, some of which will come and go the rest of your life? He does not do so in order to hold you back or tear you down. To give up in the face of suffering is simply not an option. On the contrary, suffering is the means by which he brings the greatest blessing of all into your lives. Wherever you go in life, and whatever you do, you do so as his disciples. You inherit the eternal joy of his kingdom, which transforms every blessing you receive into an infinite pleasure. Your possessions are not items of material accumulation; they are fantastic resources for enjoyment and adventure. Your family is not a burden of responsibility; it is the most precious gift ever given, cherished to the full each day. Your tasks in life are not onerous duties to perform; they are an incredible opportunity for personal growth and enrichment of life. You may carry with you the marks of Christ, but never forget their role, which is to set you apart for the best of human delights.

May God seal in our hearts and minds these lessons learned from his servant Jacob, renamed Israel, the father of all the tribes of God's people. God grant us patience and courage in every trial of life. Amen.

II

PSALM 73

The Psalms shed a powerful light on the whole of human existence. Every realm of human experience is given clear illumination from the witness of the Psalter. It is no wonder that the Psalms have continually proven an inexhaustible treasure for the daily life of the Christian. Generations of Christians have received guidance from the Psalms in every dimension of life. In our text for today, the psalmist attacks head-on a difficult question: the question of the prosperity of the wicked. Nowhere in Scripture is it more clear that the Bible has nothing to do with the "power of positive thinking." This psalm is intensely realistic in its portrayal of human folly; and yet, in the end, the glorious praise of God shines through. Brothers and sisters, hear the Word of God.

The psalm begins with a brief statement of the heart of Israel's faith. God is just in all his ways. He controls all reality according to the gracious purpose of his love. Nowhere does this psalm, or any part of Scripture, deny this truth. And yet, within the limits of this truth, the psalmist wrestles in agony with a profound question. He immediately expresses his bitter frustration, which has almost caused his entire life to go off course. The psalmist is jealous of the well-being of the foolish and boastful. They are seemingly beyond the reach of ordinary human suffering. Even in death, they seem not to suffer. They wear haughtiness around their necks like a shiny necklace; they walk around in violence like a set of clothes. The Hebrew word for violence here includes physical violence, but it also means injurious language, harsh treat-

26

ment of others — in short, every kind of rude and unfair behavior toward other human beings. The wicked do not simply make mistakes; rather, a constant and repeated pattern of abusive behavior is evident. They taunt and deride the innocent. Their speech is arrogant and demanding, delivered as if from on high. And yet they are filled to overflowing with honors and wealth. Their lives are lived in untroubled tranquility, as they go from one treacherous deed to another. And all the while they openly question the divine rule. "Relax," they say. "God isn't in control of everything. He doesn't watch our every step."

It is not an easy problem to face, but we all have to face it. How do we come to grips with the prosperity of the wicked? Several options are closed off by the witness of this psalm. The answer of the Christian faith is not to adopt an optimistic appraisal of the human condition. The Bible does not say: "Well, there is a little bit of good in everyone, so I guess I should try my best to find some good even in evil people." Such an answer flies in the face of the radical evil of which human beings are capable. Nor does the Bible say: "Maybe God controls affairs in a general way, but doesn't bother with the details of human life." Again, the witness of Scripture plainly professes the intimate involvement of God in human life and the total divine control over all reality. Nor does the Bible say: "Maybe our understanding of good and evil is too narrow. Maybe some things only look evil to me, but in fact contain some good." The Bible confesses a God who has clearly made known his will, which serves as a true and certain measure of all human behavior. The question posed by this psalm is a serious one, and it is made all the more troubling by the lack of a rationally satisfying explanation.

Just for a brief moment, the psalmist reaches the end of his rope. He comes close to throwing up his hands in hopeless resignation. He admits that he almost concluded: "If that's the way it's going to be, I might as well stop worrying about doing the right thing. If the wicked are going to prosper, I'd better join the crowd. All I've gotten for my good deeds is a daily dose of misery and suffering." He comes close, but he quickly realizes that to reach such a conclusion would be to cross a line that he must never cross. To reach such a conclusion would be a direct contradiction of Israel's faith. But then, what is the answer? The question of the prosperity of the wicked has become almost unbearable. And then it hits him. He has not reached an answer because he has not rightly asked the question. The problem is that he is thinking to himself about God. But the solution can be found only in encountering God himself directly. When he enters the sanctuary, the light of God's presence solves his problem.

The message of the Bible is absolutely clear and certain. And yet it does not yield its treasures lightly. A response of faith is required if we are rightly to discern the wisdom that it contains. The truth of Scripture does not obey the established laws of human logic. It is not given for the purpose of theological debate. The bread of life contained in Scripture is given, not to the full, but to the hungry. The waters of eternal life that Scripture holds are poured out, not for the satisfied, but for the thirsty. Now, what does this mean? Situations of human suffering are not a mistake. God himself puts us in circumstances that stretch our faith to the very limit. But he does not do so in order to hurt or devastate us. He does so in order to teach us the truth of his eternal will for our lives. It is in situations of suffering that we come to realize astonishing truths about life that were otherwise completely hidden from us.

The psalmist stops talking about God and starts talking to God. He tells God the insight into human affairs that he has suddenly realized. God is no fool; he watches every step. The psalmist sees the final destiny of the wicked, despite the temporary successes that they enjoy. The steps of the wicked looked totally secure; but in fact they are treacherous and slippery. The wicked are suddenly and entirely consumed in destruction by the divine wrath. In a single instant, sheer calamity is brought upon them. In a brief moment, they go from boastful self-assertion to complete terror. The triumphant life of the wicked is like a terrible nightmare; when the nightmare is ended, and God awakes from sleep to judgment, the very image of the wicked is disdained by God himself. In the light of God's presence, the psalmist has realized that the wicked are not at all beyond the reach of divine control. On the contrary, in his own time, and in his own way, God holds the wicked to account for every word and deed.

The twentieth century has yielded rich examples that confirm the truth of this Psalm. The wickedness of human beings has spread across the earth, in the forms of fascism and communism. There were doubtless times in which it appeared that nothing could stop their advance. They moved from victory to victory, bringing treachery and savage butchery wherever they went. The lives of good men and women were sacrificed to stop them. Battles were lost. But the war was won. In the end, both fascism and communism were totally defeated. What is fascism today but a horrible memory of a terrible ordeal for the world? What is communism today but a universally despised exercise in human tyranny and corruption? The existence of sin and evil are nowhere denied in the Bible. And yet even sin and evil are under the divine control. Even sin and evil serve God's sovereign purpose of love for the lives of his people.

The Psalm ends with an expression of exalted joy in the praise of God. The psalmist wonders how he could have been so foolish. He asks, "How could I have missed the truth? I was so completely overcome by jealousy toward the wicked that I closed my eyes to the reality of God's eternal love for me." According to the psalmist, the mercy of God, which forgives and restores to wholeness, is not simply a theological possibility. It is a reality, which has a profound and immediate impact upon all of life. Indeed, the psalmist bases his entire existence upon the truth of God's undying love. God's eternal care has been constant and active. God's guidance has accompanied his whole life in every respect. He lives in the hope of eternal glory. In sheer exhilaration he proclaims his total allegiance to God: "Whom have I in heaven but thee? And there is nothing upon earth that I desire besides thee." Not even death itself is a threat, for the power of God will overcome it. "My flesh and my heart may fail, but God is the strength of my heart and my portion for ever." The ultimate comfort is that nothing can separate the psalmist from the presence of God, whose love is eternal and all-encompassing.

Brothers and sisters, I would guess that none of us here has escaped the dilemma posed by our text today. We have all at times fallen into the trap of getting so bothered by the successes of the wicked that we forget, even for a moment, the incredible gifts we've been given. But this psalm is a challenge for you to keep something firmly in mind. God has put you exactly where the light of your lives will shine the brightest for his eternal glory. He has led you by his Word and Spirit in the decisions of life, so that costly mistakes were avoided and fruitful directions were opened up. In your lowest moments, he has not turned his back on you. Rather, he has eased your burdens and increased your enjoyment of life. He helps you to accomplish in life more than you ever thought possible. When you fall into the trap of self-pity — and which of us doesn't from time to time — remember to leave judgment to God. He is not mocked or fooled. But also consider the amazing gifts of life that you have been given. God has ordered the entire universe with one purpose in mind: to bring into your lives the full abundance of his compassion. So great is the mystery of his everlasting love.

III

FROM THE GOSPELS

1. John 3:1-21

We begin today a series of sermons based on several passages, each of which is taken from one of the four Gospels. Each of the passages contains the encounter of Christ with an individual person; we will consider one passage each week. I am not much one for titles, but we will call the series "the shape of discipleship." Our focus throughout will be on the light that is shed by each of these encounters on the living reality of Christian discipleship. Some familiar figures will be encountered, including Zacchaeus, the woman at the well, and the rich young ruler. In each instance we will seek to discern the true content of the call to discipleship as it comes to us through the example of these individual characters. We begin today with the figure of Nicodemus. Brothers and sisters, hear the Word of God.

John gives a quick description of Nicodemus, yet the brief description communicates volumes. He is a Pharisee, a religious leader of the Jewish people. In the Gospel of John, the Jews represent the world of darkness that is hostile to God's gracious purpose. So already, even before the encounter takes place, the reader is set on edge. The danger that is signaled is highlighted by the time of day of his visit; he comes under the cloak of darkness, which emphasizes the need for concealment in an atmosphere crackling with antagonism. But Nicodemus does not launch into a personal attack; instead, he does his best to assure Jesus of the respect in which he is held by the Jewish people. They have observed the miracles Jesus has performed; in John's Gospel the encounter with Nicodemus comes right after the wedding at Cana. Nicodemus addresses Jesus on grounds that are familiar to him; he calls him Rabbi, a term of great respect and distinction, and asserts that he is aware of his divine mission as a teacher of God's people. He affirms the divine origin of the deeds that Christ performs. But as occurs on numerous occasions in all four Gospels, Jesus will not meet Nicodemus on Nicodemus's own terms. Jesus does not struggle against him; he simply refuses to meet him on those terms. Instead, he gives totally new terms, the only terms upon which Christ can truly be known. "A person must be born again." The Greek word used is ambiguous; it can mean either "from above" or "again." But either way, the accent is clear; the life of genuine Christian discipleship is a radically new basis for human life, which results from the miracle of God's wondrous presence.

We must quickly recognize that, despite the centrality of this passage in the Bible, it is distorted both on the theological left and on the theological right. The left ignore it altogether; the Christian life, they say, is a natural part of human self-discovery. In their view, the very notion of a miraculous transformation of human existence is a legacy of ancient supernaturalism. Their neglect of the passage is tied to a broad cultural-political agenda of human self-improvement. The right, on the other hand, have turned the passage into a religious-political cause. To be "born again" means to vote a certain way, to adopt certain cultural and educational attitudes, and to embrace a variety of conservative programs. Both left and right have directly denied the clear implications of the text by politicizing its content. Neither discerns the astonishing truth contained in the answer of Christ to Nicodemus.

The kingdom of God is a present reality. Already, Jesus Christ rules the entire universe in unlimited freedom and eternal glory. No event occurs outside of his sovereign control. No movement of human history circumvents his loving purpose for the whole of creation. Even evil is subject to his gracious design. But against both left and right we must assert that a response of faith is required if his rule is to be understood rightly. You cannot find it through a political cause; you cannot find it through a personal or cultural agenda. It can be found only in a totally new orientation of life, in which everything that you have and everything that you are is given over to his service. The new birth of Christian discipleship is not a helpful guide to solve problems in life that may come up; it is an entirely new basis for human existence, which transforms every decision that we make and claims for itself every purpose and plan that we conceive and carry out.

Nicodemus is completely undone. He expresses in sheer bafflement his utter confusion concerning the point that Jesus is making. "How can a man be born if he is already old?" Once again, Jesus ignores the terms of the question as they are stated by Nicodemus. Instead, Jesus extends the insight he is communicating. The new life of Christian discipleship is the miraculous gift of God's Spirit, signified by the water of baptism. The old is left behind, and the new is all encompassing. It is not a question of a process of improvement; rather, it is an entirely different basis for human living through the presence of God's Spirit. Jesus appeals to an analogy to make clear the truth of his statement. The effect of the wind is easily discerned in the rustling of the grass and the trees; yet the source of that effect is unobserved by human senses. So too, the Christian life brings a palpable change in all human behavior, and yet the source of that transformation lies in the secret purpose of God.

Again, Nicodemus stammers out a question: How is all this possible? But Jesus will not give in; in fact, he goes on the offensive. How can Nicodemus not understand these matters? Is he not a distinguished teacher of Israel? Christ has come from God to proclaim the truth of God, yet the Jews have not accepted his witness. How can they understand anything, if they do not understand the whole basis for the Christian life? And how can they know anything, if they do not know that Christ himself is the Son of God, sent by God to bear witness to the truth for the whole world? Jesus Christ is the truth; his Word therefore is self-validating.

Consider today your baptism. You were baptized into the Christian faith, as a visible sign of your unity with the exalted Lord. The water of baptism signifies the complete change of life that results from your participation in the death and resurrection of Christ. You now live by God's Spirit, not by the ways of the world. Every dimension of your life has been transferred from your own purposes to the purpose of Christ for you. The way you relate to your family and friends, the service that you extend in the fellowship of the church, the way you spend your time and resources in the many tasks of life — your whole being is claimed from above by Christ himself, who will not settle for half measures or partial fulfillment. This is not a matter of arcane Christian doctrine; it is a basic issue of the Christian life, without which no true knowledge of Christ is possible.

Jesus finally opens the floodgates, and the full truth comes rushing out. Christ must be put upon the cross to die, just as the serpent was once held aloft by Moses. Belief in the saving death of Christ on the cross is the exclusive basis for receiving the eternal benefits of the gospel. Why? Because God gave his Son to die for the sins of the world, in order to achieve the eternal purpose of his redeeming love for all humanity. Whoever believes in Christ will not be condemned, but will inherit the eternal blessing of the gospel. The purpose of his coming was not condemnation but salvation for the whole of creation; those who refuse to believe are already condemned because they fail to receive the free gift that is being offered to everyone in the gospel. Why are they condemned? Because Jesus Christ himself is that light by which the entire universe is brightened. Whoever withdraws from him, withdraws into the darkness of evil. Those who withdraw from Christ do so in order to conceal the evil in their deeds, which Christ's own light exposes and corrects. In contrast, those who remain with Christ do so because their deeds in life are performed through God himself. They do the truth, and they therefore abide with the truth.

Brothers and sisters, the cross of Jesus Christ draws a clear and distinct line. The way to God cannot be found through efforts of human self-justification and self-righteousness. The gospel is the message of God's free gift of eternal love, which can be received only in the wide-eyed wonderment of child-like faith. It does not call for "commitment"; it calls for a total change of life, which receives every blessing with utter astonishment and glee. It does not result in "good deeds"; it results in radical obedience to the imperatives of the gospel, which breathe life and joy into every aspect of human living. However wise and understanding we may become, we never outgrow the need to hear the truth of the gospel. God so loved the world: a child can understand it, yet the wisest person that ever lived can never learn it deeply enough.

2. Mark 10:35-45

We continue today our series of sermons on the shape of Christian discipleship. Our series is focused upon several encounters of Christ with various people in the Gospels. We are especially concerned with the help these passages give us in our own attempt to be faithful to the call of the Christian life. We began last week by considering the figure of Nicodemus. We noticed the challenge of radical change that accompanies the profession of faith. We observed the sheer newness of the life of faith, through the energy of God's Spirit. Today we consider a second encounter, this time the exchange that takes place between Jesus and two of his disciples: James and John. Once again, our effort is to discern the subtlety and richness of true service to Christ. Brothers and sisters, hear the Word of God.

Let us begin by setting the scene. James and John are two of the twelve apostles, whom Christ has called into special relationship with himself and with his ministry. But even within the narrow circle of the twelve, these two, along with Peter, clearly have an unusual closeness to Christ. These two brothers, children of Zebedee, are the first disciples whom Jesus calls; remember how they were out fishing, and Christ commanded them to follow him, and he would make them fishers of human beings. And again, when Jesus is transfigured and appears momentarily in his true glory, this takes place in the presence of these two disciples and Peter; Christ had taken them with him apart to the mountain to behold his exalted state. Later on, when Jesus goes to the garden of Gethsemane to pray, it is again these two disciples and Peter that he takes with him, to share his burdens. James and John are close to the center of Christ's ministry all along the way. We must also stress in setting the scene that the event takes place just prior to the passion of Christ. Jesus is poised to enter Jerusalem and knows the fate that awaits him there. He has already foretold his death to the disciples, but they have misunderstood his statement. According to Mark, they are afraid to ask Jesus to clarify what he means.

James and John approach Jesus with a question, in fact a request. They begin by inquiring whether he will fulfill their petition. The effect of this initial step is to make clear the respect and devotion in which they hold him. They would not come to him with the request that they do, unless they already know that he and he alone is in a position to meet it. Their motives are pure, even if in the end their request is refused. But at this stage, Jesus simply asks them: "What is it that you want me to do?" Again, their question already assumes the coming glorification of Christ: their request is that they be allowed to share in that glorification in the closest possible way. Jesus' initial answer uncovers their failure to come to grips with his own purpose in coming. His glorification is tied to a cross; his exaltation is closely bound to his own death. They see only the one side of the paradox and not the other. But they insist that they really do understand, and Jesus relents. But still, he refuses to meet their request. The reason is clearly stated: the role of particular disciples is grounded in the secret and eternal purpose of God's election.

The Gospels do not hide the frailty and vulnerability of the disciples. Indeed, the overwhelming emphasis of the Gospel of Mark is upon the inability of Jesus' disciples to comprehend his true identity and mission. The example of the disciples is instructive for us, for we, too, share in the struggle of faith to understand and to obey the commandments of Christ. Everyone here has done and said things that we wished had never happened. The example of the disciples is surely an indication that we ought not to be too hard on ourselves in the day-to-day affairs of Christian service. When we make mistakes, the answer is not a barrage of self-doubt and self-torment. Instead, we should remember that we are not the first to make mistakes; even the nearest followers of Jesus, upon whom he called in his own times of need, often stumbled in discerning his true purpose. We should put our mistakes behind us and move ahead, seeking insight from our mistakes into the true content of God's will for our lives. The struggle of faith is never easy; and yet the eternal treasure that we find in our striving is well worth every effort that we make.

The remaining ten disciples hear about what has occurred, and they react with anger; they are indignant that such a request has ever been made at all. But Christ quickly cuts off such a reaction. Instead, he immediately turns the issue into a general principle that affects the lives of all the disciples, and not just James and John. What is at stake for everyone is the very substance of following Christ. A comparison is made with the usual order of things in the world. There, those who wield influence and authority over others abuse that prerogative in order to tyrannize their fellow human beings. In sharp contrast, the way of the world is turned upside-down among the company of Christian disciples. Here, the true measure of leadership is in terms of the service rendered to the common fellowship. The greatest of Christian disciples is not the most influential, but the most effective in giving aid for the genuine welfare of others. Christ not only stresses the true content of the life of discipleship; he also clarifies its genuine basis. The shape of discipleship is determined by the One whom every disciple follows: Christ himself. Discipleship is service, because Christ himself came in order to serve humanity through the giving of his life as an atonement for sin.

Augustine was once asked to describe the Christian life, and he answered in three words: humility, humility, and humility. Humility knows that the greatest gifts in life do not come in places where awards are handed out, but wherever the excitement of shared purpose glows. Humility recognizes that the best of times are had in ordinary living, not in artificial and manufactured happiness. Humility realizes the profound joy that even the simplest of gifts can bring into the lives of others, and it is ever ready to do even a little in order to bring delight and encouragement. Humility transforms even small pleasures into infinite gains by the joy of living that it always possesses. Humility passes over regrets without a glance or murmur; it seizes and magnifies every moment of time shared with others. Humility overlooks the mistakes of others — who has not committed the same faults? — and embraces every sign of reconciliation in human affairs. Humility does not call attention to itself; instead, it bends over backwards to highlight the generosity and thoughtfulness of others.

Our text today is instructive for the Christian life; but it is also helpful in describing the basic attitude of the gospel in relation to ecclesiastical power and influence. The gospel never celebrates centers of power and influence in the church; it always attacks them, whether on the left or on the right. It was so in the early church, when the fathers struggled against the widespread heresies of Gnosticism and Arianism that swept across the landscape of ancient Christianity. It was so at the time of the Reformation, when Luther and Calvin struggled against abuses in the late medieval Catholic Church. It was so in

Germany during the War, when the confessing church resisted the tyranny and brutality of official Nazi policy. The issues change over time, and so do the resources the church brings to bear upon them. But what stays the same is the basic posture of the gospel toward heresy, however dominant and deep-seated. The gospel never attacks persons; it only attacks positions. But attack the gospel must, or it is no longer the gospel.

Brothers and sisters, I have no need to tell this congregation about the nature of Christian service. If I do, it is only to remind you of what you already know and exhibit every day. I have never been in a church in which the true nature of Christian discipleship is more clearly seen than here. It is reflected in the eager and attentive service rendered by your treasurer, your clerk of Session, your music director and choir, your organist; it is easy to see in the care and devotion to duty in your Session and committees; it is ever present in countless deeds of kindness and mercy on the part of individual members of the congregation. Let us be encouraged to remember that God sees every unnoticed act of obedience to Christ and that he places infinite value especially upon those deeds that are unknown to others. According to Christ, those deeds which we perform in his service apart from public acclaim will bring an eternal dividend. "Your Father who sees in secret will reward you" (Matthew 6:4).

3. Matthew 19:16-22

We continue today with our series of sermons on the shape of discipleship. Thus far we have considered the story of Nicodemus and the approach to Jesus by the disciples James and John. We have recounted the newness of the Christian life and the humility that it bears in all circumstances. Our focus today is upon the encounter of Jesus with the rich young ruler. The exchange is recorded in all three synoptic Gospels: Matthew, Mark, and Luke. While different notes are accented in each Gospel, the basic theme of the passage is held by all three in common. There is no doubt that the story of the rich young ruler is a challenging text. Its explosive content is overwhelming in proportion. Sadly, the history of church exegesis has found a series of maneuvers to soften the text; however, the sheer power of the truth that it contains refuses to be neglected or ignored. Brothers and sisters, hear the Word of God.

Mark gives an inviting description of an eager young man who hastily approaches Jesus as he is about to leave on a journey. The young man runs up, kneels down, and presents a question: "Good Teacher, what must I do to inherit eternal life?" (Mark 10:17). Two things are to be noticed about the question. First, the form of address the young man uses is unusual for the time. However, there is nothing to suggest that he was trying to flatter Jesus or that he thought of him as more than an ordinary human being. Second, the content of the question was a common concern of pious Jews, taken from the Old Testament itself. How do I gain entrance into God's eternal presence? How do I secure a place in God's kingdom? In Matthew, the question posed is similar: "What good deed must I do to inherit eternal life?"

Now, in both Matthew and Mark Jesus rejects the question as framed by the rich young ruler. Instead, he reframes the question and answers it on a new basis. He does so for different reasons in each Gospel; and yet the effect of his rejection is the same. In the canonical form of Matthew's text, Jesus replies: "Why do you ask me about what is good?" In the context of the Old Testament, it is already well known that to ask about the good is to ask about God himself. God has made known his will to his people, and the fulfillment of that will is required of all who seek him. The good is not a matter of philosophical debate but of concrete action. In Mark, Jesus replies: "Why do you call me good?" Jesus rejects the form of address because it infringes upon the goodness of God. God alone is the source from whom all goodness derives and to whom complete obedience is owed. God has revealed his will in his commandments, the doing of which insures eternal life. Jesus does not answer the young man's question. Instead, he restates the truth of the Old Testament, which is the proper theological context for the question.

The church has time and again fallen into the trap of answering the rich young ruler's question directly, rather than reframing it. Instead of observing the clear logic of the answer that Jesus gives — by refusing an answer — the church has time and again gone on the defensive in relation to the ethical strivings of the world. It waits for the world to ask questions; then it rushes to the scene, pretending to have the answers ready-made. It tells the world what it wants to hear — whether liberal or conservative — then stands back and waits for the world's approval; then it moves on to whatever issue is next raised to the surface. In our own time, this discussion is conducted in the language of so-called "values," but the fact is that every age of the church has seen different words for the same error. But in thus going on the defensive, the church has failed the mission of the gospel. The role of the church is not to answer the world's questions. The role of the church is to teach the living will of God, which is the only hope of true life and joy for all humanity. The gospel is always on the offensive, never on the defensive.

Moreover, it is crucial to see the full implications of Jesus' initial answer to the rich young ruler. We are accustomed in the Christian church to reading the Old Testament as part of the inheritance of our faith. And indeed, we are also used to turning from the Old Testament to the New, hearing the witness of the Old in the light of the New. But the answer of Jesus to the rich young ruler brings to light a depth dimension that is often missing in the church's understanding of Scripture. We are also to return to the Old Testament itself as a living witness to the person of Jesus Christ. Christ ignores the question of the rich young ruler because it fails to recognize the continuing authority of the Old Testament, not simply as a source of questions, but as a source of answers. The Old Testament cannot be understood apart from the person of Christ, who is its true reality; and yet, neither can the person of Christ be understood apart from the Old Testament, which bears truthful testimony to him.

Mark's Gospel makes clear that the young man won't give in yet. He tries to push the issue one step further. "Teacher," he says — at least he's learned one point Jesus has made — "all these commandments I have observed from my youth." The implication is, What do I still have to do? The real issue of the encounter is now brought to the surface. The young man agrees that God's commandments reveal God's will, which is the way to life. He is not insincere, nor does he lack religious devotion. Mark emphasizes the point by stressing that Jesus took him in his gaze and felt great affection for him. But then Jesus gives the concluding response: "You lack one thing; go, sell what you have, give to the poor, and you will have treasure in heaven; and come, follow me." Now, Protestants have often argued that Jesus is making the demands of the Law impossible, in order to illustrate that salvation is by faith rather than through works of the Law. Traditional Catholic exegesis assumes that Jesus was adding to the Law, to show a way of higher righteousness for Christians that is better than the Old Testament. Finally, there are numerous modern psychological interpretations, which suggest that Jesus is trying to illustrate for the young man the nature of human commitment. However, none of these interpretations is supported by the text itself. The central point is that Christ's answer does not add another commandment to the Ten Commandments. Christ's answer is not a general moral principle, but a concrete imperative to this young man. The purpose of his response is to put the whole will of God into proper perspective for the young man, who has failed to understand the challenge of concrete obedience in sheer abandonment of all else. The young man is not lacking a piece of information concerning God's will; he lacks any understanding of God's will at all, because he has not loved God with his whole being.

The same conclusion is reached in Matthew's Gospel, only along a slightly different path. There the conversation takes a somewhat sharper turn, when the young man asks which commandments he should keep. Jesus answers by reciting from the Ten Commandments, and adds the final summary concerning love of the neighbor found in Leviticus 19:18. The point here is that the Law is not a series of legalistic propositions. Rather, love of neighbor is the intended purpose of the Law from the very beginning. Jesus does not intend to contrast an older ethics of the Old Testament with an enlightened morality of the New. Instead, he adds to his answer: "If you would be perfect, go, sell what you possess." This is not a state of higher moral perfection. It is the basic requirement of the Old Testament, that God's people are to be perfect, even as God himself is perfect. The goal of the Law is to transform God's people into his image, which is holiness. Just like in Mark, the issue does not concern an additional requirement beyond the Law; rather, it concerns a proper understanding of the whole point of the Law from the beginning, which is to fulfill the obligations of love. In both Matthew and Mark, the young man withdraws, because he feels he has too much to lose.

Brothers and sisters, the problem that every Christian faces throughout the whole of life is the problem of the human will. God's will is not a mysterious unknown; it is not concealed in the realm of human values, which only distort and pervert its true content. God's will is made known in his commandments, which are to be obeyed. The purpose of these commandments is not to set us apart from everyone else in a state of moral superiority. The purpose of these commandments is to teach us how to love God with total surrender in every dimension of our lives. If God's will seems unclear or uncertain, the problem does not lie in its biblical expression. The problem lies in us. God's revealed will is absolutely perfect and complete, and without fail leads to fullness of life in God's presence. But the path it sets out before us can be seen only if we take the steps of concrete obedience. The incredible paradox of Christian ethics is enduring: only those who obey God's commandments understand his will; and only those who understand his will obey his commandments.

4. Luke 19:1-10

We continue today our series of sermons on Jesus' encounters with various people in the Gospels. Today we take a somewhat different turn. Nicodemus was a well-known religious leader; James and John were extremely close disciples of Jesus; the rich young ruler was a devout follower of Jewish tradition. But Zacchaeus is none of these things. Suddenly, on the road that passes through Jericho, Jesus comes upon a human being without the sterling credentials of those we have already met. Indeed, because of his occupation, Zacchaeus starts out with two strikes already against him. A new theme is sounded in the exchange between Jesus and Zacchaeus, which gives essential help in our own understanding of the Christian life today. Brothers and sisters, hear the Word of God.

Jesus is on his way to Jerusalem, and he passes through the town of Jericho. The stories of the Gospels are not myths or images, but set in the context of real life at a specific time and place. A second character is quickly introduced; as in the case of Nicodemus, the introduction is short, and yet it contains an enormous amount of information. Zacchaeus is a tax collector — in fact, he is the chief of the tax collectors — and he is rich. In the first-century Roman empire, tax collecting was not a systematically regulated enterprise. Some tax collection was assigned to private contractors; they paid a specified sum to collect certain taxes in a specific area, and then they tried to make a profit on the transaction. The result was a great deal of fraud and extortion, which gave the whole occupation a bad name. Even Christ himself refers in the Sermon on the Mount to tax collectors as a group of notorious sinners: "Do not even the tax collectors do the same?" (Matthew 5:46). Even worse, Zacchaeus is the head of all the tax collectors in his region. He has amassed a considerable fortune farming out the tax collection responsibilities in the area around Jericho. But perhaps worst of all, Zacchaeus is a Jew. Tax collectors were hated by Jews, as a sign of Roman domination; yet here the representative of Roman rule is himself a Jew. And Jesus is walking right into his neighborhood.

But before he arrives, Zacchaeus himself gets ready for Jesus' appearance in the town of Jericho. He is very eager to find out more about Jesus. The text gives no particular motive for his interest. However, it clearly spells out his high degree of anticipation and enthusiasm. His interest compels him to get close enough to actually see Jesus as he walks by; no one wants to be on the outside looking in, unable to see something worth seeing when it comes this close. But he faces an obstacle; he is a short man and is simply not able to see above the massive crowd that gathers around the figure of Christ on his way down the road. Zacchaeus doesn't give up; he turns necessity into a virtue. He races ahead of the moving throng and finds a good shade tree in the exact path where Jesus is headed. He climbs the tree and awaits Jesus' arrival.

The story of Zacchaeus is a clear indication of the proper relationship between the Christian church and the world. We do not approve the misdeeds of the world; indeed, we are frankly realistic about the radical evil that exists in the world. And yet, our role is not to form an alternative universe, which excludes everyone evil. Whenever the church has tried such a tactic, it has inevitably created more problems than it has solved. The habit of Christ throughout his ministry was to eat with the wayward and the immoral — so much so that he was known as a "friend of tax collectors and sinners." The church has always gone wrong when it has tried to become more righteous than Christ himself. What is at stake is not the nature and extent of human sin; that is a wholly different question and deserves a full and clear answer. What is at stake is the way the church relates to the world of sinners. The church is not to withdraw from them; it is not to exclude them; in fact, it is to share with them in the many blessings of life.

Zacchaeus's plan works well enough up to a point. But little does he know that an entirely new dimension will soon be brought to his efforts. Jesus eventually comes to the place where Zacchaeus is perched in the tree, waiting for a glimpse. He looks up into the tree, and there is this little man, gaping down upon him. Jesus does not hesitate at all; he tells Zacchaeus to come down as quickly as possible, for it is essential that he stay in his house on his visit to Jericho. The Greek word leaves no ambiguity; what is at stake here is not a prearranged convenience, or a welcome diversion; it is required by Jesus' very mission that he come and stay in the house of Zacchaeus, the head of all the tax collectors in the district. The response of Zacchaeus is immediate; he hastily descends from the tree and extends his hospitality to Christ as a guest in his home.

The call of discipleship is seldom a confirmation of well-laid plans and long-cherished dreams in life. Discipleship does not add the finishing touch to what is otherwise a completed structure of life-endeavor. The challenge of faith does not come when we expect it and have prepared well in advance to receive it. The call of service to Christ breaches what are otherwise noble life projects. The claim of obedience to Christ tears down the structures of life endeavor and rebuilds in their place the unimaginable designs of divine purpose. The invitation to follow Christ demands a response, which cannot be delayed without losing the astonishing opportunity that it opens up. There is no substitute for the eager obedience that characterizes the Christian life. Reluctance, distraction, and procrastination are not an option for true response to the summons of Christ.

The story continues by sharply contrasting two different reactions to the command of Christ to Zacchaeus: that of the crowds following Jesus on the one hand, and that of Zacchaeus on the other. Within an instant of finding out what has happened a buzz begins to stir through the gathered mass of people. Once again, it is said, Jesus has crossed a line that he ought not to cross. He is openly associating with the wrong kind of person, and he is even willing to accept his offer of overnight lodging. For the crowds the reaction is much the same as it has been often enough before. But for Zacchaeus, nothing will ever be the same again. The change in his life is instant and overwhelming. He rises and solemnly addresses Jesus face-to-face; he pledges to him that he will give half of all he owns to the poor; and he states that he will make a generous return to any whose income he has expropriated unjustly. In fact, the act of restitution is found in the law of Moses itself: "If a man steals an ox or a sheep, and kills it or sells it, he shall pay five oxen for an ox, and four sheep for a sheep" (Exodus 22:1).

The response of faith transforms in a palpable way the whole of human existence. When unbelief encounters the call of discipleship, it goes on as it always has before. Nothing really new takes place; the reality of Christian proclamation is simply subsumed under the well-established customs of dealing with human affairs. But for faith, the content of Christian proclamation effects a total and lasting alteration of human life. Old habits, however cherished and useful, are put aside. Old ideas, however widely shared and convenient, are forgotten. Old dreams, however glittering and appealing, are left behind. The call of discipleship does not enhance the given elements of a human life; it seizes that life from above, changes it forever, and sets it out in a new direction. From then on, the one thing that matters, above everything else in the universe, is to do what Christ commands. It does not matter what popular opinion says; what matters is that God himself has spoken.

Jesus follows the response of Zacchaeus with an incredible statement of his own. The encounter between himself and Zacchaeus is the point at which redemption breaks into the life of Zacchaeus. Jesus clearly extends his complete approval to the pledge of Zacchaeus. Zacchaeus has rightly understood the divine command, and his response of obedience makes him fit as a child of father Abraham himself. And then comes the conclusion of his statement, and the whole point of the story itself. The change of life in the sinner Zacchaeus is not an incidental occurrence in Christ's otherwise busy schedule. The exchange between Christ and Zacchaeus is the very purpose for which Christ came into the world: to rescue lost sinners and to render their lives whole again.

Brothers and sisters, the universal church all too easily loses its bearings on the question raised by our text today. Those on the left simply deny the reality of sin, which is clearly contradicted by the total change in Zacchaeus's behavior. Those on the right seek to exclude sinners, which again is contradicted by the very action of Christ himself. But however widespread the confusion of the time in which we live, the summons of Christ is clear. It is not your prerogative to deny the fact of sin, which Scripture everywhere condemns. Nor is it your duty to expel the sinner, as the crowds wish to do. You must hate the sin; but you must also love the sinner. And who knows what astonishing results may come about? For Zacchaeus, the sinner, is now a beloved child of Abraham.

5. John 4:1-42

We continue today our series of sermons on the shape of discipleship. Thus far, the encounters we have studied have all involved Jewish people. This fact confirms the primary focus of the earthly ministry of Christ, which was limited to God's chosen people Israel. But today we come upon an exception to the rule: a lengthy and subtle exchange between Christ and a Samaritan woman. The story of the woman at the well is one of the richest in detail of all such stories in the four Gospels. It is also rich with insight into the nature and purpose of Christian discipleship today. Brothers and sisters, hear the Word of God.

Samaria is a block of land located between the province of Judea in the south and the province of Galilee in the north. In the time of the New Testament, Samaria was considered a "no-man's land" by pious Jews. The inhabitants of this area were scorned as substandard in respect to the promises and laws of God contained in Scripture. John carefully records the occasion upon which Jesus ventures into Samaria. The pharisees, who have already expressed enormous hostility to Christ's ministry, have become aware of his popular success. In order to avoid the expected step-up in pressure, Jesus decides to relocate from Judea to Galilee. But on the way he has to pass through Samaria. He arrives at a town called Sychar, the site of a well-known well. Traveling in ancient times was extremely laborious — presumably Christ was on foot — and Jesus arrives at the well under a noon sun worn out from exertion.

The disciples of Christ have gone on into the town itself to pur-
chase provisions. But Jesus is not alone at the well for long. A woman
arrives, a Samaritan woman, to draw some water from the well. Jesus
requests that she use her water jar to draw out a drink of water for him
as well. The woman is instantly suspicious: Why is this man, who is
obviously a Jew, willing to associate on such friendly terms with a Samaritan? She repeats the well-known fact that Jews and Samaritans go
out of their way to avoid each other. But Jesus quickly reverses the
question. If the woman only knew the identity of the one who asked
her for water, she would have sought from him, and he would have
given her living water. But the woman's suspicion persists and causes
her to misunderstand. She points out that Christ has nothing to draw
with; she mockingly asks whether Christ has a source of water that is
greater even than Jacob's own well. But Jesus immediately clarifies her
error. The water to which he refers is not this water — which refreshes
only for a moment — but water given by Christ himself, which satisfies
eternally.

The gospel breaks down the walls that divide human beings one
from another. It breaks down the wall of rich and poor; the Christian
church welcomes within its doors every human being, regardless of
economic status, and urges upon all a basic concern for the welfare of
those who are in need. It breaks down the wall of male and female;
Christian marriage is a unity of affection and shared enjoyment of experience between a man and woman, which forever changes their
whole perspective on life. It breaks down the walls of race; prejudice
against other human beings because of the color of their skin is a clear
sign that the message of salvation has not been properly understood. It
breaks down the span of human generations; parents delight in the
growth of their children, and children treasure the wisdom of their parents. Where the gospel is rightly received, the ordinary customs of division between human beings are turned upside down.

The woman is finally convinced that something worth having is being offered to her; so she asks, simply, to be given this everlasting water.
Once again, Jesus takes the initiative and tells her to summon her husband and return with him. The woman gives a guarded reply: "I have no
husband." But Jesus himself exposes the full truth. The woman has already gone through five marriages, and she is now living with a man out

of marriage. The woman began with a suspicious attitude and saw only the surface meaning of Christ's words; then she realized what he offered and expressed her desire to have it; now she sees his omniscient power and calls him a prophet. She draws ever closer, but still is confused: Jews worship in Jerusalem, she insists, but Samaritans worship at their own holy mountain. And still Jesus persists: he tells her that a day is soon to come when true worship will be limited neither to Jerusalem nor to Samaria. There is a difference between Jews and Samaritans, for Jewish worship is given by God, and true salvation comes from the heritage of the Jews, not the Samaritans. But in the time to come, true worship will not be limited to Jerusalem; it will take place wherever the Spirit of God dwells and will be authenticated by the truth that it contains. The woman moves one final step closer toward understanding. She says that she has heard about the coming of the Messiah, and she understands that his knowledge is unlimited. But then Jesus himself gives to her his own final word: "I who speak to you am he."

The day of which Jesus spoke has come with the dawn of the Christian church. Christ the risen Lord sent forth his Spirit to dwell within all who confess his name. Within the church, too, walls are broken down. No denomination has a monopoly on the truth. Whether Lutheran, Methodist, Baptist, Church of Christ, Pentecostal, Presbyterian, Episcopalian, or Roman Catholic, every denomination has made some contribution to our universal understanding of the content of our faith. As we say every Sunday in the Apostles' Creed: "I believe in the holy catholic church." The source of the unity of the universal church is the true identity of the One whom we worship: Christ the Lord. In the Presbyterian Church that unity is expressed by the fact of an open table for communion; the invitation to celebrate the Lord's Supper is extended to all baptized Christians who desire to partake.

At this point in Christ's conversation with the woman of Samaria, the disciples return from the town, while the woman leaves to tell her fellow citizens what has happened. The disciples clearly see that custom is being overturned by what is taking place, but they hold their peace. Instead, they tell Jesus it is time to eat. Once again, Jesus uses a routine occurrence as an occasion for communicating an astonishing truth. He informs them that he already has food that they know nothing about. They wonder among themselves: How did he get it? But he tells them plainly that what sustains him is to do God's will at all times, until the very end. He uses a figure to reinforce his point: some are saying that the harvest is still a few months off; but in fact the fields are already full of ripe grain, ready to be picked. Those who bring in the harvest are gathering for eternal life, and they will receive a rich reward. The end result is unbounded joy for both sowers and reapers, for both have shared together in the labor of the crop. The disciples are reminded that others have sown the seed, which they themselves now bring in.

The growth of the church is a mystery, grounded in the sovereign purpose of God for salvation. Lasting growth does not come through planned programs of extension; it comes through the witness of ordinary Christians, like yourselves, whose daily lives reflect the reality of the Christian faith. Church growth is not grounds for boasting, as if size and success always go hand in hand. Instead, it is grounds for sheer, unbounded gratitude. The very reason you exist in the world is to testify to others by your words and deeds of the One whom you serve. Church growth is a miraculous divine gift, which confirms in human experience the gracious purpose of God for the whole world. It is not cause for self-congratulation; but it is cause for celebration, in recognition of the wondrous gift that has been given.

The woman has been led from a minimal grasp to a close encounter with the truth. The disciples have learned an invaluable lesson about the nature of Christian witness. But still, the climax of the story has not been reached. The true climax occurs with the return of the woman together with several people from the nearby town. They are drawn to Jesus because of the witness of the woman. But when they arrive, they come to genuine faith through their own hearing of Christ's word.

Brothers and sisters, we are not of the first generation of Jesus' disciples. We do not meet him face-to-face in his earthly life. Rather, it is through the apostolic testimony — through the writings of Scripture — that we encounter the risen Lord himself. By the presence of his Spirit he opens our ears to hear his voice in the pages of the Bible. The words on the page are not lifeless relics from antiquity; they are the sure and certain guide to God's eternal will for all humankind. In them, we hear him; and hearing, we believe.

6. Mark 14:3-9

We conclude today our series of sermons on the shape of discipleship. So far in this series we have encountered a wide variety of people to whom the call of discipleship is extended by Christ himself. On the one hand, the enormous variety of human personality and circumstance is not suppressed by the gospel. Each of these characters is so realistically portrayed that one would not be surprised to meet them on the street. And yet, on the other hand, the result of the encounter with Christ is in no sense an exercise in human self-understanding. The call of discipleship is radical, all-inclusive, and absolute in its claim upon human life; it leaves open only the simple response of obedience, or the sad fact of withdrawal from Christ.

Our final entry in this series concerns the anointing of Jesus by the woman. All four Gospels record the event, though there is considerable variation in their accounts. The canon of Scripture makes no effort to smooth over the variations in the Gospels, and neither will we; rather, our focus will be upon the common theological witness that is made, even despite numerous differences in detail. What do we learn about the person of Christ from the account of his anointing? And what do we perceive about Christian faith from the surprising deed that the woman performs? Brothers and sisters, hear the Word of God.

The Gospels are agreed that at one point in Christ's ministry a singular event occurs, which evokes a heated response. The event involves a particular woman: in Mark and Matthew she is nameless; in Luke she is called a sinner; in John she is identified as Mary, the sister of Martha. All agree that an anointing of Christ takes place. However, one difference is paramount: exactly when the anointing of Christ occurred. Matthew, Mark, and John locate the anointing of Christ just prior to his entry into Jerusalem. For these three Gospels, the incident serves as an introduction to Jesus' passion. In Luke, a similar description occurs at a different time, and for a different purpose. We will keep Luke's text in mind; but our focus will be upon the other three. For these Gospels, the encounter provides the transition to Christ's crucifixion.

In Matthew and Mark, the scene is set in Bethany at the home of Simon the leper, while in John it takes place at the home of Lazarus.

Mark sets down the hostile general climate at the time the event occurs: the scribes and the Pharisees are already plotting to put Christ to death. As Mark tells it, Christ is dining at the home of one Simon of Bethany, who suffers from a terrible skin disease. While Christ is eating, a woman approaches. She carries in her hand a special alabaster flask used to carry precious ointment. Such a flask would have had a long neck, which would be broken off when the contents were used. She breaks off the neck and pours the expensive perfume contained in the flask upon the head of Jesus. Other Gospel accounts present different features: in John, she anoints the feet of Jesus and wipes them with her hair; in Luke, she openly weeps and washes the feet of Christ with her tears and kisses them. But all the Gospels agree that the perfume is a costly gift, and John adds that its fragrance fills the entire room.

Our text depicts the sheer beauty of Christian discipleship. The anointing of Christ by the woman dramatically portrays the honoring of Christ with all of one's costliest possessions. The service we owe to Christ is not a half-hearted matter, which one can easily take care of in one's spare time. The claim of discipleship surrounds all of life and evokes a total response. In particular, the Christian faith does not shield us from the struggles of life. There are griefs to be borne that often seem beyond our capacity to endure them. But the amazing fact is that such times do not take us farther away from Christ; in truth, they draw us nearer to him. Is it not so often the case that in the midst of difficult times we gain a clearer understanding of the wisdom of his will? Do we not, in the midst of suffering, often receive a fuller vision of his compassion for all humankind? The mysterious paradox of the Christian faith is that our deepest suffering is encompassed by Christ's own love and transformed into fresh devotion to his service.

The Gospels record the reaction of others who are there witnessing the event. Mark speaks of the general response by those who see what the woman has done. They express their displeasure and disapproval of her deed: "Why was so much expensive perfume wasted in such a useless manner? Surely it could have been sold for a large amount of money, and the proceeds distributed to the needy." Matthew focuses upon the insensitivity of Christ's own disciples. They, too, see what the woman has done, but they can do no better than join in the general reaction of the crowd in censuring her act. Finally, John focuses upon one individual response in particular: that of the betrayer, Judas. He, too, attacks the woman's gesture as a profligate act, which has deprived the poor of needed aid. John also carefully records the motive of Judas, lest any reader misunderstand: "This he said, not that he cared for the poor, but because he was a thief, and as he had the money box he used to take what was put into it" (John 12:6). Mark summarizes vividly the overall response; those who see the woman's act literally snort out their disdain.

We could not pass a single day without the wonderful support of family and friends. There is no more precious gift from God than the kind words we receive in difficult moments and the sharing of fun and joy with others in the pleasures of life. However, we must also remember that the service of Christ cuts across all human ties and binds us directly to the person of Christ himself. In the final analysis, his commandments are the highest priority in life, and they cannot be ignored without terrible loss. It is easy to lose our bearings, easy to be consumed by worry about the good opinion of others, even of those we love most. But in the end, we are not accountable to anyone else for our actions. Service to Christ is an incredible freedom, which breathes energy and purpose into every endeavor that we undertake. We must not give in when that freedom is threatened; instead, we must remember where our ultimate loyalty rests, and from whom we receive true fulfillment in life.

In sharpest possible contrast to the general reaction is the reaction of Christ himself. He not only refrains from offering criticism of the woman; he goes out of his way to praise her deed, and in fact points out its true significance. The woman must be permitted to do her work, and she is not to be bothered by unfair blame. The common opinion that her act has deprived the poor of needed help is a sheer smoke screen. The needs of the poor are an ongoing concern; but this woman, says Christ, has performed a unique and irreplaceable service, fully warranted by the circumstances. She has anointed his body for burial. She has prepared him for the passion that he is about to undergo, which will bring salvation for the entire world. She has anticipated the future by her own act of spontaneous love. Because of this service, her deed will be recorded, and it will be remembered wherever the message of redemption is preached.

What is the best measure of Christian discipleship? What is the surest way to determine the will of Christ? Now, it is clear that there are times when you have to do the right thing, even when it is a burden. No amount of inner resistance releases you from the obligations of love that Christ himself puts upon you. But it is still safe to say that the best way to find the path that Christ himself would have you follow is to do what brings you greatest enjoyment in life. If you are overwhelmed, then perhaps it is time to limit the range of your responsibilities. If you are listless, perhaps it is time to seek new challenges of mind and body to pursue. The astonishing fact is that emotional well-being is not tangential to Christian faith; it is embraced by God himself, who made us whole creatures, and who keeps our entire existence as his intimate concern.

We conclude now, brothers and sisters, our series on the shape of discipleship. Only a few of the vast cast of characters in the Gospels have been considered, not to speak of the even larger cast in the remaining portions of Scripture. The significance of these stories is twofold. On the one hand, the reach of the gospel extends to the whole of the human race; the will of God revealed in Scripture is eternal and universal in its scope. But on the other hand, the Bible does not render Christian truth in a series of static propositions that can be stated in abstraction from the human life they illuminate. The light of the gospel is so powerful that it leaves no dimension of human experience in the shadows. The gospel's light brings what is concealed to the surface, and it puts into proper perspective what is confused or troublesome. And the gospel comes with the promise that those who live by its light will perform deeds of lasting significance, which outlive any other human design.

IV

PSALM 27

One of the greatest challenges to the life of Christian discipleship is the fear of suffering. Whether it is in the form of illness, or adversity, or grief, or other difficulties in life, the Christian faces along with everyone else periods of trial and even agonizing hardship. As with every other dimension of life, the Psalms do not skirt the issue of fear; instead, they confront it head-on. The Psalms are intensely realistic about human existence and do not conceal even for a moment the real conflicts that the faithful must endure. However, the Psalms also go out of their way to show the proper theological context in which such afflictions are to be understood, and they describe the right attitude in which the servants of God are to face them. Let us consider today the witness of Psalm 27. Brothers and sisters, hear the Word of God.

The opening verses express the basic conviction of this psalm, and of the entire Psalter, and indeed of the whole of Scripture. God is the source from whom every blessing in life is received. He is the measure of every truth affirmed, and the goal of every hope cherished. The God of heaven and earth reaches down directly into the life of the individual and meets every need with his unlimited resources. If that is true, what basis in reality is there for timid anxiety about the hardships life may bring? God has been the constant means of safety, protection, and refuge from every conceivable danger in life. He has shielded the psalmist from every possible harm that has arisen. If that is true, what reason is there to live in constant dread? The psalmist proceeds by describing his experience of the attacks of his enemies. When enemies begin their determined assault upon the psalmist, they are the ones who stagger and collapse. Once again the psalmist communicates his confidence: even though an entire army should come up against him, he will not lose his nerve. Even if war is openly declared, he will maintain his steady calm. And the reason for his confidence is his recognition of the infinite superiority of God over every danger, however great it might appear.

It is often said that there is no real point in worrying, because we cannot control events anyway. Why be anxious about what we cannot change? There is certainly a note of truth in this sentiment, and it does find a place in the range of witnesses in the Bible. Jesus himself said that we ought not to worry, for we cannot lengthen our lives by even one single hour. But still, we must dig a little deeper if we want to find the rich treasure of insight that Scripture has to offer on the question of fear. The basic truth upon which Scripture rests its testimony is that God is truly in control of every event and every circumstance in life. God does not simply paint the big picture but leave the details untouched. On the contrary, the grand purpose of God in the creation of the universe is expressed in his attention to the details of the world he has made. God does not give us merely a general idea of what the Christian life is all about and then leave us to fend for ourselves. He actively intervenes in daily life, in order to bring us joy and delight.

The psalmist continues by stating his own goal in life. When all is said and done, one thing stands above everything else: that he may remain forever in the presence of God. His intense desire is to gaze forever upon the beauty of God himself, which is the highest form of human fulfillment. The one object of his effort in life is reflection upon the content of God's eternal will. And he realizes that God himself has made this enjoyment possible. When conditions have become burdensome or unmanageable, God has removed the psalmist, as it were, to a hiding place, free of danger. The word used here is "booths," the same word used to describe the temporary shelters Israel inhabited to commemorate the flight from Egypt. God has treasured the psalmist in his own keeping and established him in a place of total security. The result is that the psalmist, and not his enemies, receives the victory. As a consequence, the psalmist pledges himself to offer gifts of joy in the Tabernacle and to manifest his delight in songs of exuberant celebration.

God does not simply give us a helping hand when we find ourselves in trouble. He puts us in a time and place where every aspect of reality contributes to our growth and insight into his goodness. He surrounds our lives with more beauty than a hundred lifetimes could fully appreciate. He brings around us such expressions of kindness and encouragement that everyday existence is filled with the deepest satisfaction. He transforms routine living into endless excitement, with an untold variety of thrills. Through the miracle of his presence, obligations become fantastic opportunities for enrichment; duties in life become a noble calling, bringing unbelievable contentment; indeed, life itself becomes an astonishing adventure of discovery in the knowledge of God. Fear of hardships simply gives way to the eager embrace of God's many blessings in life.

The psalmist now turns from theological reflection upon the marvelous ways of God to direct address of God himself in prayer. The content of his prayer makes clear that the confidence of the psalmist is not to be confused with an easy optimism. The answer of faith is not simply to close one's eyes to danger. Rather, the answer is to appeal to God to remove the danger. The psalmist reminds God that the desire for God's presence has been the guiding thread of his whole life. He asks God to extend into the future the help he has always provided in the past. He pleads that God will not thrust him away or keep him at a distance, for the presence of God is life itself. Again, the psalmist is fully aware of very real dangers to human happiness. He mentions one in particular, which stands as a symbol of every possible threat. What if a person were abandoned by his own parents? What if a mother and father were to turn against their own child? Even such an event, however inexpressible the anguish it would cause, would not prove the undoing of faith. Even if he loses the love of his parents, God himself will care for the psalmist as his very own. Above all, the psalmist requests that God will make known his will, and that the course and fortunes of his life will unfold in a place of safety, comfort, and prosperity. The psalmist knows that his enemies spread malicious rumors and breathe out violence. And so he asks God to shield him from their wicked schemes.

The easiest thing in the world to do is to overreact to dangers that we face. Now, the Bible would not have us ignore dangers, as if they do not exist. Simple positive thinking accomplishes nothing and has nothing to do with faith. Dangers are real and can pose a supreme threat to our very well-being. The wise Christian will take those dangers seriously. However, despite the need to do what we can, the fact is that most threats appear all the more menacing because there is nothing that we can do. Here is where the risk of faith is crucial. On the one hand, we can spend our time worrying ourselves sick about possible outcomes and waste our energy dreaming up alternative plans. Worst of all, we can put one of those plans into effect — and probably make matters much worse than they already are. Or we can ask God to keep us and our families from harm and focus our time and energy upon doing the things that God has given us to do. Often enough, the storms of life pass over without damage. But even when they strike close to home, we are reminded of the practical steps of the Christian life and the transcendent peace that governs the whole of Christian existence. When danger comes near, do what you can; but don't panic.

Psalm 27 closes with a brief exhortation. The only possible basis for joy in life is steady confidence in the eternal care of God. Any other basis is simply unthinkable. And so the psalmist encourages his readers to stand firm in unbreakable courage and to depend upon God, whatever the trial.

Brothers and sisters, the Bible does not guarantee that you will never face trials. On the contrary, it plainly states that you will, not just once but on various occasions throughout your life. Indeed, it even suggests that Christians often seem to be a special target for adversity. You cannot deny the danger; nor do you have the power to put your fears to rest once for all. One of the hardest achievements of faith is the courage to carry on with life, even when troubles are near. It will take every ounce of self-restraint that you can summon, with God's help. But it will bring in return a whole new world of appreciation for the overwhelming compassion of God.

V

FROM THE LIFE OF SOLOMON

1. 1 Kings 2

We begin today a series of sermons based on the figure of King Solomon, the third of Israel's kings. The account of King Solomon is given in the first eleven chapters of 1 Kings. The overall perspective of 1 and 2 Kings is clearly communicated within the books, which constitute part of the former prophets. The material they cover is actual history, so real that the reader is constantly invited to check with other sources to confirm the truth of their witness. And yet the history is told in such a way as to lay bare for the reader the divine purpose that governs this amazing series of events from the beginning. That purpose is clearly given in the book of Deuteronomy: when Israel obeys the revealed commandments, it will receive the manifold divine blessing in all aspects of life; when it disobeys, it will receive the divine curse. The reign of Solomon begins in the blessings of obedience; during his lifetime, Israel flourishes in ease and prosperity. However, as an old man Solomon departs from the Law of God and opens the gate to havoc and devastation upon Israel after his death. Over the next few weeks, let us consider in detail the story of Solomon. Brothers and sisters, hear the Word of God.

The reign of Solomon follows that of his father David, who reigned after Saul. Solomon's reign does not commence without a struggle. When David is near his death, another of his sons, Adonijah, the son of

Haggith, sets himself up as king over Israel. Adonijah has the help of the commander of the army, Joab, and the priest, Abiathar. But David undercuts Adonijah's arrogant pretensions, just as he once did those of Absalom, and establishes Bathsheba's son, Solomon, as king. Our text today begins with the final encounter of David with his successor to the throne, Solomon. He speaks as a father to his son, but also as one royal generation to the next. He tells Solomon that his own end is near and commends upon him utmost vigor and courage in his duties. He admonishes him to observe diligently the clear promise of divine care: if Solomon will obey fully the Law of God revealed to Moses on Mount Sinai, then his every endeavor will bring abundant success. In fact, his obedience will confirm the special promise of God to David: to establish from his heirs an everlasting kingdom.

The Law that God revealed to Moses on Sinai, which has at its heart the Ten Commandments, is the eternal rule by which every human life is measured. As if to reinforce the comprehensive scope of its claim, our text stresses that even Solomon, the king of Israel, is subject to the Law of God. We are not prophets, and so we do not have the right to stand in judgment over human history. But as Christians, we are subject to the truth of which the prophets speak. No human being who ever lived or who ever will live is above the Law of God revealed to Moses. The Ten Commandments are with absolute certainty the perfect expression of God's living will for the whole of human life. They are a truthful guide to life in the joyous presence of God. But they also mark out the fatal way of removal from the blessed inheritance of God. As Jesus said, "till heaven and earth pass away, not an iota, not a dot, will pass from the law until all is accomplished" (Matthew 5:18).

With the passing of generations from one ruler to the next, it is also time for David to settle some old scores. Long ago, Joab, as commander of the army, had exceeded his rightful authority and used his position to carry out a personal vendetta. His murder of Abner and Amasa was not a necessary military operation, but a private bloodbath motivated by a struggle for power. His unlawful action cost the lives of two good and revered men. So David tells Solomon that Joab must pay for his crime. On the other hand, David exhorts Solomon to extend his protection and hospitality to the family of Barzillai the Gileadite. When David was fleeing for his life from Absalom and had to leave Israel behind for the wilderness, Barzillai brought much-needed food and provisions for David and his supporters. Such personal loyalty, David tells Solomon, is never to be forgotten. And finally, David instructs Solomon to carry out vengeance upon Shimei, who cursed David as he fled from Absalom. David admits that he once swore to Shimei that he would not harm him, despite his curse; but he now tells his son Solomon to exact revenge for the deed. After these final words to Solomon, David dies, and his glorious reign of forty years comes to an end.

Now, the first two accounts to be settled are fully in accord with the overall perspective of Scripture. First, Joab has committed an egregious offense. He has abused his office to afflict injury upon the innocent. His killing of Abner and Amasa is outright murder, because it is not sanctioned by the limits of just war. It is a blatant war crime, and as such it must be punished. Second, the reciprocal loyalty that Solomon owes to Barzillai is a clear instance of the Hebrew concept of *chesed*, which is usually translated as kindness. To show *chesed*, or kindness, is to carry out obligations that are implied by certain human relationships. Fulfillment of these obligations is not considered by the Old Testament as a matter of charity, to be granted when the occasion permits. Rather, they are a sacred duty, which only the wicked and perverse ignore. Are we not bound, even today, to the observation of David's advice? Do we not reckon as utterly reprehensible the abuse of power to afflict the innocent? And do we not embrace as essential to the Christian life the fulfillment of our obligations to those entrusted to our care? Kindness toward others is a requirement incumbent upon all who would live life according to God's design.

But now we come to the third of these scores, that of Shimei. The text makes no effort to comment upon the ethical dimensions of David's request. But surely here as readers of Scripture we must step back and consider his command in the light of Scripture as a whole. David had made a sacred oath to Shimei that he would not harm him. To make such an oath is to invoke the imperative of the third commandment: "You shall not take the name of the Lord your God in vain" (Exodus 20:7). Is it not a sheer evasion of this commandment to circumvent his oath by passing along the vengeful deed to his son? Has he not in doing so violated his own vow to Shimei? Not even King David, a man after God's own heart, seems aware of the distortion of God's will that he is committing. And what does that mean for us? Surely at the very least that personal revenge is an unreliable indicator of the proper course of action. Pent-up anger harbored against others only clouds our objectivity and drains away the carefree enjoyment of living. Holding a grudge, in the end, will only lead us astray. Forgive, and forget, and move on to fresh blessings to come.

The text immediately relates how far Solomon has taken to heart the advice of his father. He begins his reign with resolute action. First, he sees through the underhanded scheme of his former rival, Adonijah. Adonijah tries to manipulate the relationship between Solomon and his mother, Bathsheba, asking Bathsheba to persuade Solomon to give him the hand of Abishag in marriage. Abishag the Shunammite was the nurse of King David toward the end of his life. But Solomon instantly sees through the plot, for a marriage of Adonijah to Abishag would be a powerful symbol of Adonijah's claim to the throne. It would in fact amount to a capitulation to Adonijah's effort to usurp the royal title. Solomon decisively stamps out the threat before it even has time to unfold. Second, Solomon banishes Abiathar the priest, withholding the death penalty only because of Abiathar's former allegiance to David. Third, Joab is executed, and Benaiah is put in his place as commander of the army. And lastly, Shimei is put under house arrest; when Shimei breaks the terms of his incarceration, he is executed as well.

Thankfully, brothers and sisters, we do not have in our country the political system that once governed ancient Israel. In a democracy, former rivals are not put to death; instead, the popular majority guarantees the smooth transition of power from one administration to the next. But despite the foreign political system under which he served, it is still crucial to learn from the nature of Solomon's initial activity. One of the greatest threats to the life of faith is indecision. It is a sheer illusion to think that a mature faith spends time mulling over the options and then, having found the best one, proceeds hesitantly. In fact, the opposite is true. When once the proper course in life is clear, the right approach is to forget once and for all the dreams of the past. There is a necessary boldness to faith, which seizes opportunities and makes the most of them. When God shows you the path to take, no matter how unfamiliar the ground, leave everything else behind and take it. You will never regret it.

2. 1 Kings 3

We continue today our series of sermons based on the figure of King Solomon. We began last week by observing the transition of power from the rule of David to the rule of Solomon. We focused upon David's declaration to Solomon of the need for total obedience to God's commandments. And we considered the resolute action of Solomon in seeing through the deceptive action of his rival, Adonijah, and in carrying out the directives of David concerning his enemies. We pointed out the vast difference between the political system of ancient Israel and our own, and yet affirmed the need to follow the example of Solomon in our own daily lives, by walking without fear or hesitation the path in life that God paves before us. In our text for today, Solomon faces the task of confronting a new era, different from the period of his father David, with a different set of problems to solve. How will he solve them? Brothers and sisters, hear the Word of God.

The text begins by painting a general picture of the times in which Solomon lives. David's reign was a time of conflict in which David led the people of Israel in glorious battle against their enemies. His first emergence onto the scene was his own hand-to-hand fight with Goliath the Philistine, and the astonishing victory he won was repeated time and again throughout his reign. Because of David's incredible career, the time of Solomon begins in an atmosphere so far foreign to Israel: it begins in peace. Solomon commences his reign with a marriage alliance to the Pharaoh of Egypt, by marrying the Pharaoh's daughter. Every reader of the Bible knows the extraordinary leap of diplomacy this entails, for the Egyptians were once Israel's mortal enemies. Moreover, the text describes the different role that Solomon must play. For David, the primary focus was upon defeating the enemies of Israel. Israel's very existence was at stake. But for Solomon, the primary focus is upon building for the future of Israel. The text stresses that Solomon undertakes his duties with full devotion to God. However, it also states the immediate problem confronting him at the outset: the absence of a central place of worship in Jerusalem.

It is remarkable how crucial the role of timing is in the Christian life. The needs of the church change over time. Actions that were indispensable in one age may no longer be appropriate in the next. Issues that were paramount at one point may have given way to a very different set of priorities at another point. The gravest threat to the church in this instance is to face new challenges with the old set of solutions — to fight battles that long ago lost their purpose, or to apply tactics that no longer help the overall strategy. Where are we in the church today? Despite the period of intense confusion through which the church has passed, have we not turned a corner in the life of the church? Despite the constant need to defend the boundaries of the church's confession on the left and the right, is not the primary task of the church in our time to build for the future? Is not the proper focus of the church's witness the practical affairs of ordinary Christian existence? Is it not time to recover for a new generation insights into the language of faith that were once second nature to every Christian, but are now a foreign language to large segments of the church?

God appears to Solomon one night in a dream. He asks Solomon an amazing question: What would you like me to give you? Solomon answers, first, by expressing his gratitude for the kindness of God shown to his father David. The Hebrew word for kindness here is the same word we mentioned last week: *chesed*. As we saw last week, human beings show *chesed,* or kindness, to one another by fulfilling the obligations of their relationships. But here it is clear that even God exercises *chesed*, or kindness, toward his children. Because David obeyed the commandments of God with eager obedience, God gave him total victory over his enemies; and above all, God gave him an heir to his throne. But Solomon confesses to God his complete inadequacy to meet the tasks of leadership that he has been given. God's people are a vast company, and Solomon tells God of his own utter inability to make the decisions that will be necessary. He asks God for wisdom to guide God's people.

God responds to the request with complete approval. He affirms that Solomon has made the right matter the highest priority. Solomon has not asked for a long life; he has not asked for the defeat of his enemies; he has not asked for an abundance of wealth. Instead, when given the opportunity, Solomon has put at the top of his list the desire for wisdom in the conduct of his God-given duty. And God grants Solomon's request. He gives him the wisdom that he desires, so much so that Solomon outshines every other human being by his knowledge

63

and understanding. And indeed, God also gives to Solomon the wealth and honor for which he did not ask, so that Solomon's reign is superior to all the surrounding kings. And finally, he promises him a long life, if he will obey the divine commandments as his father David did. The dream ends, and Solomon wakes up; he returns to Jerusalem to offer sacrifices and holds a feast for his servants.

The church at large is constantly harassed by so-called prophets, who would tell us God's will concerning everything under the sun. Whether on the right or on the left, they would tell us who to vote for, what good causes we must adopt, what prepackaged programs we must install. But these are false prophets, and they are the last thing the church needs. The wise Christian will simply ignore their folly. Instead, the church needs men and women of wisdom. Wisdom recognizes and accepts the limits of the church's responsibility and action. Wisdom sees the needs of the time and does not try to retreat into the past. The very foundation of wisdom is radical obedience to God's revealed will, without anxious concern for the passing fads of this world. Wisdom receives every dimension of life as a gracious divine gift and seeks to draw from every gift the greatest possible enjoyment. Let us not fail to ask, in order that we might receive.

It is not long before Solomon's discernment is put to the test. Two prostitutes approach the throne with a case. One woman presents her side of the story. She and the other woman live together in the same house. Both have just given birth to children. Only a few days after the birth, the two women were alone in the house for the night with their newborn babies. One night, the other woman, she says, snuffed out the life of her own infant by lying on top of it. Moreover, during the middle of the night she secretly exchanged her dead infant for the living one of her house companion. The woman states that when she woke up in the morning, she discovered that her baby was dead. But then, after she examined the child more closely, she realized that a substitution had taken place. The dead child was not her own. After the first woman finishes her story, the second woman gives her own. She denies outright that an exchange has taken place. The living child, she states, is hers, while the dead child is her companion's. Again, the first woman sticks by her story.

Solomon quickly sizes up the situation. First of all, it is not a question of failure to communicate. There is a clear difference of irreconcilable opinion. One is right, and the other is wrong. But which is which? Once again, the decisive quality of Solomon's action asserts itself. He calls for a sword to be brought and gives the command to sever the living infant in two, giving one piece to each of the two women. For the real mother of the child, the very thought of such a deed is completely unbearable. Her motherly affection for the child is overwhelming, and so she immediately relinquishes her rights to the child in order to preserve its life. Above all, she says, the child must not be killed. But the deceptive woman goes along with the king's plan. "Sure," she says, "that's a good idea, and it will certainly solve the issue between us. Go ahead and divide it in two." King Solomon quickly commands that the child be given to its true mother and repeats her emphatic statement that the child must not be killed. The ruling that Solomon gives is instantly broadcast around the kingdom, and Solomon is held in enormous respect for his shrewdness.

Brothers and sisters, by acting as he does, Solomon does not claim for himself omniscience. He does not claim to know what no human being can know. Instead, he seeks to provoke a reaction, through which the truth will be clear for everyone to see. Neither can we see into the hearts and minds of other human beings. However, if a course of action is undertaken in deception, sooner or later the deception will be uncovered. Plans undertaken in defiance of God's commandment will in the end be defeated. Apart from God's revealed will, human wisdom, however clever and ingenious, becomes the ultimate folly. And so also, on the other side of the coin, the good deeds of the Christian will shine like the mid-day sun. Don't be afraid to do what is right, even if it is momentarily misunderstood. God himself will bring every good work into the light of his eternal glory.

3. 1 Kings 5

We continue today our series of sermons based on the figure of Solomon. Thus far we have witnessed the transfer of power to Solomon from his father David. We observed Solomon's prayer for wisdom to guide him in the great task he is given to accomplish. We saw how Solomon applied that wisdom in a particularly difficult situation, and we noticed the public approval that resulted from his solution to the problem. In our text for today, we turn to the work that will occupy the major part of Solomon's entire reign: the building of the Temple. Up until now, Israel has had no Temple, though the Temple is described in the Law of Moses. But to Solomon is given the fantastic assignment of bringing the plan of the Temple into reality. Let us consider the steps that he takes and the insight that his action yields for the Christian life today. Brothers and sisters, hear the Word of God.

The fourth chapter of 1 Kings, the chapter previous to our text for today, gives a brief summary of Solomon's reign as it begins to unfold. It is a time of incredible happiness for the still young kingdom: "Judah and Israel were as many as the sand by the sea; they ate and drank and were happy." The sphere of influence that Solomon's rule commanded was greater than at any other time: "Solomon ruled over all the kingdoms from the Euphrates to the land of the Philistines and to the border of Egypt: they brought tribute and served Solomon all the days of his life." The text goes on to describe the wealth of the kingdom, and gives a beautiful picture of the freedom and contentment its inhabitants enjoyed: "And Judah and Israel dwelt in safety, from Dan even to Beer-sheba, every man under his vine and under his fig tree, all the days of Solomon." Solomon's wisdom is praised, and his role as the author of well-known proverbs is mentioned: "For he was wiser than all other men . . . and his fame was in all the nations round about. He also uttered three thousand proverbs; and his songs were a thousand and five." In short, it is a glorious time for the people of Israel under the leadership of a wise and accomplished king.

At once, Solomon sets out upon the task that will constitute the heart of his life's work: the building of the Temple. He receives some emissaries sent by Hiram, the king of the Phoenician port city of Tyre, located just to the north of Israel. Hiram was a contemporary of David and Solomon and already had a long history of trade with Israel. The text mentions the personal loyalty and affection that Hiram felt for David, which he now clearly wishes to extend to Solomon as well. Solomon immediately recognizes an incredible opportunity and proposes a deal. He reminds Hiram that David had been unable to build the Temple because of the necessary battles for survival in which his reign was embroiled. But now that peace and prosperity have come, Solomon tells Hiram, he intends to carry out the directive of God given to David: that his son would be the one to build the Temple. And so Solomon proposes an exchange: building materials and the skill of Hiram's laborers in return for agricultural products from Israel. It is a clever deal in which both sides benefit; for Israel, a young kingdom, lacks the technical expertise required for a major building project, while the Phoenician seacoast city lacks developed land. In particular, Solomon requests of Hiram that Phoenician loggers cut the necessary timber, for their know-how is legendary.

We do not all have the same tasks in life. Solomon's commission was different from that of his father David; and God gives each of us a different calling, with unique duties to perform. But several things are underlined by the example of Solomon in the performance of his duty. First, he uses the very best resources at his disposal. When we carry out the assignments we are given, there is no point in going only halfway. If something is not worth doing well, it is probably not worth doing at all. A good goal in life is worth every effort that we put into it. Second, Solomon wisely sees the work that he has been given by God to do and gives to that work his exclusive attention. For every one of us there are a thousand and one temptations that could distract us from doing the jobs that need to be done. But Solomon puts his energy full-force into the project that he knows he is to accomplish. And finally, there is the bold decisiveness by which Solomon undertakes his labor. Everything else is dropped in order to fulfill the purpose in life that God has given him. There is surely no greater feeling in all the world than finding your niche in life, knowing that you are in the right place at the right time, and doing what you enjoy most. The whole world may pass by as it will; but doing God's will is infinitely greater delight.

Hiram hears Solomon's proposal and consents wholeheartedly. He quickly realizes that Solomon possesses all the wisdom of his father David, and he gladly agrees to the proposed exchange. Hiram develops a plan for delivering the needed supplies to Israel. His loggers will cut down the trees, with the help of labor supplied by Solomon. The trees will be transported to the seashore, where they will be used to construct rafts. These rafts in turn will be floated down the coast to Israel, where they will be broken up, and the wood carried inland. The Phoenicians were expert sailors, so Hiram's plan brilliantly combines the skills of his workers. The plan is set in motion. Hiram supplies as much wood as Solomon requires, while Solomon gives Hiram in return a large quantity of wheat and olive oil. Once again, the text reminds us, Solomon's action confirms the divine gift of wisdom and the divine blessing of peace during Solomon's reign.

How do we know what tasks in life God would have us to do? Surely every Christian goes through times in which this question is unclear. And we have doubtless all made mistakes along the way trying to figure out where in life to put our time and energy. But our text for today gives us a helpful clue. Through the mystery of God's care for the universe that he has made, he supplies each of us with interests and abilities that set us apart from every other human being. The key here is to go with your strengths. Those things that you do best in life are probably a good indication of where your efforts will be the most fruitful. Don't be bothered that others may have different strengths; thankfully, the accomplishments of others are only a source of stimulation and encouragement for your own work. Instead, pour everything you have into the things in life you do best, and the results will be well beyond your every expectation.

The chapter concludes by describing the labor force that Solomon gathers in order to carry out the necessary work of building the Temple. It is a fantastic undertaking, a marvel of organization and logistics. Thirty thousand men are grouped into three units of ten thousand each, which work in shifts that shuffle back and forth between Israel and the wooded mountains of Lebanon. Another seventy thousand are assigned to general duty for transport of raw material. And another eighty thousand are sent to help cut the timber. Solomon chooses a chief officer to oversee the enterprise, Adoniram, who works with a corps of 3,300 deputies to manage each phase of the project. Finally, Solomon directs huge, expensive stones to be quarried and shaped for the laying of the foundation of the Temple. His own stonecutters join with Hiram's to carry out the task, which involves precise craftsmanship.

Now, there is unmistakably a note of ambiguity in this final description of Solomon's preparation for building the Temple. Long ago, when Israel first began to cry out for a king in order to be like its neighbors, the prophet Samuel warned the people of what would happen: "These will be the ways of the king who will reign over you: he will take your sons and appoint them to his chariots and to be his horsemen; . . . and he will appoint commanders of thousands. . . . He will take your menservants and your maidservants, and the best of your young men . . . and put them to work" (1 Samuel 8:11-12, 16). Despite the divine blessing of the kingship in Israel, the predominant tone in the former prophets is decidedly against monarchy. Even a king as wise as Solomon uses forced labor. Does it not give us pause to consider today what an incredible privilege it is to live in a democracy?

But on the more positive side of this final section, brothers and sisters, is the clear emphasis upon the creativity and enthusiasm with which Solomon sets about his work. He carefully deploys all his resources and sets in motion the dream of a lifetime. When we find the right path in life to take, it is no time to hold back anything in reserve. When the time is right, we ought to commit all the resources we can find to do what needs to be done. When it is time for caution, the better part of wisdom is to await developments and bide our time. But when it is time to act, it is essential to use every last ounce of imagination and vitality that we possess. To do our best at what God has given us to do is an inexpressible gift. It is a blessing that drops straight down from heaven into human life.

4. 1 Kings 8:22-54

We continue today our series of sermons on the figure of King Solomon. We saw last week how Solomon began work on the project of a lifetime: the building of the Temple in Jerusalem. He arranged with Hiram, the king of Tyre, to supply raw materials and skilled labor. And with Hiram's indispensable help, over a period of several years, the Temple is built. It is an elaborate and glorious structure, combining grandeur with precise and intricate craftsmanship. In our text for today, Solomon has the people of Israel gather together for the purpose of dedicating the Temple. The Ark of the Covenant containing the Ten Commandments is brought to the new Temple. Solomon pronounces a solemn recital of the events that have transpired. And then he offers a prayer of dedication. Let us consider the content of his prayer and the instruction it offers us in the Christian life today. Brothers and sisters, hear the Word of God.

Solomon's prayer is a public prayer, the function of which is to draw the whole of Israel into grateful response to the living reality of God. He begins his prayer by extolling the uniqueness of God, beside whom there is no other god in the entire universe. The astonishing character of God is manifest in the loyalty and kindness that he shows toward his people Israel, who serve him with their whole being. And in particular, God has made known his identity through his accomplishment of his promise to David, his promise of a son to build the Temple. God declares his wonderful purpose, and he does what he says he will do; such is the great mystery of his infinite goodness. Solomon continues by asking God to fulfill his promise to David of a perpetual heritage to sit upon the throne of Israel.

The source of every good thing in life is the loving-kindness of God, who does what he promises. His gracious will is not limited to the restrictions of human circumstance; for he who created the whole universe from nothing also creates new circumstances, which far exceed every conceivable human plan. His care for human life is not bound to the ordinary flow of routine custom. The One who rules all history intervenes directly in human life, in order to accomplish his loving purpose for our welfare. His design for the future is not held back by the mistakes of the past. There is no direct line from the past to the future, for standing over both is God himself, who puts our past behind us and paves the way of our future before us. The total reality of human existence is subsumed under the care of God, who directs the whole of creation according to his purpose of love for his people.

Solomon professes his wonderment at the divine concern for human life. But then Solomon acknowledges an amazing paradox: though God himself has commanded the Temple to be built, and even though the glory of his presence has already filled the Temple, nevertheless God cannot be contained in any structure fashioned by human hands. God does not owe Israel anything. Instead, the requests that Israel brings to God are based exclusively upon the sheer mercy of God, who has chosen to encompass Israel within the sovereign reach of his love. For this reason, the chief act of devotion that Israel owes to God is prayer. God's gifts do not fulfill obligations; they are free gifts. And he wants to be asked, in order that Israel might receive. Solomon asks that the Temple be the earthly sign of God's presence, toward which private and public prayers are offered to God. And he desires that God would hear and answer those prayers.

There is a necessary tension in our understanding of the Christian church. On the one hand, we believe with all our heart that God has chosen this one people, out of all the peoples of the earth, for himself. Before he made a world independent of himself, God called us each by name. And the very reason for which he made creation was to bring into our lives eternal blessing. The Christian message of salvation is the one hope for the whole world. But on the other hand, God has not withdrawn his concern for the rest of his creation. He who rules over his people also rules the vast extent of human affairs in every detail. He who provides for the daily lives of his people also supplies the needs of the entire creation, human as well as nonhuman. He who gives joy and enrichment to his children also sustains profound beauty and wisdom in the world of human culture. The world of creation is not an enemy to the church; it is the theater, as Calvin puts it, in which God's eternal glory is displayed.

Solomon continues by describing the full range of concerns that Israel brings before the living God in prayer. First, when oaths are presented in the Temple in cases of dispute, God is invoked to punish the guilty and to clear the name of the innocent. Second, when Israel sins against God and is overtaken by enemies on account of their sin, and if they repent of their sins, then God is invoked to pardon their deeds and restore them to freedom in their own land. Third, when natural disasters or illness plague the people of Israel, then God is invoked to forgive their sins, to teach them the truth of his will, and to deliver them from calamity. Everyone, says Solomon, knows their own private afflictions, and God in turn knows the condition of every human being; so appeal is made for God to make lives whole again, that everyone may obey God throughout life. Fourth, when strangers enter Israel on account of the glory of God that is manifested there, God is invoked to answer their prayers alongside those of his people, in order that his name may be magnified the world over. And finally, appeal is made for God to deliver Israel from harm when Israel is engaged in battle against its enemies.

The prayer of Solomon is a beautiful testimony to the Old Testament understanding of human life under the compassionate rule of God. The presence of God fills every dimension of human experience. Human relationships are not separated from relationship to God; on the contrary, a right understanding of our relationship to God brings with it fresh insight into the true nature of human relationships. Human troubles are not foreign to the reality of God. And yet, when God brings difficulties into our lives, he does so not in order to hurt or destroy, but in order to teach and guide. God's care is extended over the whole of creation; and yet his incredible love is expressed in his intimate involvement in the details of individual lives. His peace and blessing rest upon his chosen people; and yet his kindness does not seal his people off from the world, but rather serves as an invitation for the entry of the world into his joyful presence. No reality in creation, however menacing it may appear, is a threat to God's eternal love. Whatsoever it pleases God to do, that he does; and his protection of the lives of his people is not hindered by any limitation, however many dangers may appear.

The final petition that Solomon lays before God concerns the future of Israel when it finds itself overcome by the effects of its own sin. Given the human condition, sins are only to be expected, and they will incur the full effect of divine wrath. God will hand Israel over to its enemies, who will force the Israelites into exile in a foreign land. However, if the Israelites recover their senses and seek the knowledge of God with every fiber of their being, God is invoked to forgive their offenses, to defend their case, and to cause friendly regard to be shown to them in the land of their captivity. The reason Solomon gives for God to do all of this is that God himself brought Israel out of cruel bondage in Egypt and formed it as his own heritage. He led Israel out of Egypt by Moses and adopted its people as his true children among all the nations of the world.

It is all too easy for us to be too hard on ourselves for the mistakes that we have made. The Old Testament does not present human beings as burdened down with a heavy load of guilt and endless remorse. There is a divinely established remedy for human sin. We admit to God what we have done, we change our behavior, and then we never once look back. The overwhelming freedom of the gospel is that God does not extend the mistakes of the past on into the future; instead, he creates a new future, full of fresh possibilities, and containing unlimited new resources. He does not simply give us a second chance in life; instead, he brings into being a whole new world in which to pursue the reality of his eternal design. There is nothing Christian about unending self-recrimination; it is never wise to be more spiritual than God himself.

Brothers and sisters, we no longer have a Temple; the church itself is now the temple of the living God, the place where the Spirit of God dwells. But we do still have prayer, which serves today, even as it always has, as the divine invitation to encounter the Maker of heaven and earth. Let us never neglect so astounding an opportunity.

5. 1 Kings 10:1-13

We conclude today our series of sermons on the figure of King Solomon. We have treated several episodes in the life of Solomon, which trace his accession to the throne, his request for wisdom, and his brilliant achievement in building the Temple. We have noticed the complete change in the situation of Israel that comes about in the transition from the reign of David to the reign of Solomon. Different times require different solutions, and at every turn Solomon rises to the challenge of guiding the people of Israel toward the future. In our text for today, the rule of Solomon is presented in its most glorious moment, when he receives an official visit from the queen of Sheba. The text describes the visit, which serves as the crowning event of an entire life, in great detail. Let us consider this visit and the help it gives us in understanding the life of discipleship. Brothers and sisters, hear the Word of God.

The text gives no information to prepare the reader for the stunning visit of the queen of Sheba. Suddenly, she appears in Israel. Before we describe her visit, it is worth remarking what an extraordinary alteration in Israel's fortunes is symbolized by her arrival. Until Solomon's reign, Israel was battling for its very life. It was engaged in a constant border war with the Philistines, and its history moved from one military campaign to the next. But David's victories pass on an era of peace to the new generation, and Solomon wisely uses his time and energy for long-term goals. And now the young kingdom, once embroiled in conflict with its enemies, is sought out by the foreign emissary of an established monarchy. In fact, it is not a representative who is sent, as in the previous exchange with Hiram, king of Tyre. This time, the queen of Sheba herself comes to Israel.

The text describes the occasion for her visit. She has heard of Solomon's distinguished reputation for the wisdom given to him as a divine gift. But hearing is not enough; she wants to see for herself just how true the reports are. She brings with her a number of perplexing problems to solve, and she will make up her own mind based on Solomon's solutions. Her appearance in Israel is no ordinary, routine occurrence. It is a spectacular entrance, with the larger-than-life pageantry befitting a queen. She is accompanied by an enormous entourage. She brings with her camels loaded down with spices, a huge quantity of gold, and precious stones. She wastes no time in carrying out her purpose. She approaches Solomon with every difficult matter she is aware of, and he gives her the right answer in each case. No issue in any dimension of her life is outside the scope of his illuminating wisdom.

Consider for a moment the incredible reality of the canon of Scripture. It was written and shaped in times of extreme hardship. The prophets of the Old Testament were not men of leisure, with extra time to spare in working on religious projects. They were called by God to dangerous duty, which often put them in the direst of circumstances. The apostles of the New Testament were not later historians of an event in which they did not participate. Rather, they were chosen by Christ himself to testify to his words and deeds, which they themselves had seen. Some of the greatest letters of the New Testament were written in prison. Yet this collection of writings, written by those whom even their own contemporaries doubtless considered mad, is now the greatest treasure of the church's life. In every age, it has provided the church with the one certain basis for faith and practice. It has time and again helped the church to distinguish right from wrong; it has shown the church when to stand firm and when to bend, and how to avoid dangers before they are even present. This one book contains the light of life for the whole world. It is worthy of the church's best effort to understand it.

The queen of Sheba quickly realizes that her expectations have not only been fully met, but have in fact been totally surpassed. She is simply overwhelmed. She contemplates the truth of Solomon's wise observations. She looks around and takes in the majesty of his surroundings — the dazzling architecture of the Temple, the splendid arrangements of food and service, the fine attire of the court attendants — and she is completely spellbound. She turns to King Solomon and openly admits that every rumor she has heard has turned out to be true. Now that she has seen it all for herself, she realizes that the living person is even greater than the legend. She tells him how lucky the people are who are there to hear his wisdom all the time. She pronounces a blessing on Solomon, expressing her praise of the God who made Solomon the just king on account of his eternal love for Israel. And she makes Solomon a magnificent present of the expensive items she has brought with her. The text pauses to record similar gifts of gold, stones, and fine wood given to Solomon by his friend Hiram; the wood is used to embellish the buildings and to manufacture musical instruments. Finally, Solomon returns the generosity of the queen of Sheba with gifts of his own, indeed giving her whatever she wants.

It is certainly true that God does what he says he will do. He accomplishes his promises in the lives of his people. But even here, it is easy to underestimate the amazing reality of his passionate love. I would guess that every one of us would have given up not once but a hundred times along the path of life. But God will not let us give up; he will not let us give less than our very best. When we stumble, he picks us up, puts us back on our feet, and shows us the next step in life to take. Obstacles that appear insurmountable he miraculously causes to evaporate into thin air before our very eyes. By the time we discover the real secret of our needs, he has already provided the right resources to meet every one of them. His commandments are not a burden to be borne reluctantly; they are life-giving in their purpose and all-encompassing in the truth of their content. The greatest paradox of all is that the service of God is perfect freedom.

I wish I could end this series of sermons on Solomon right at this point. But tragically, the text of Scripture compels us to move in a different direction. Despite the marvelous success of Solomon's reign, it ends in catastrophic failure. There is no mystery involved concerning its precipitous decline. Solomon is not content with a single wife, his original marriage to the daughter of Pharaoh. He eventually accumulates over seven hundred wives and three hundred mistresses, all taken from the surrounding nations. When he reaches old age, his many wives finally cause him to betray his undivided loyalty to God himself. The builder of the Temple goes on to build other temples for other gods, so that his many wives can have places of worship. The text depicts a gradual descent into open rebellion. First Solomon breaks the commandment prohibiting adultery; then he ignores the prohibition against marrying pagan women; and finally he reaches the final abomination of outright idolatry. At a stroke, everything Solomon has achieved in building up the kingdom of Israel is destroyed; a process is set in motion that will result in the end of the monarchy. God had warned Solomon of the consequences of disobedience, but he didn't listen.

When is the struggle of faith over? Is it over when you graduate from school and set out to make a name for yourself? Is it over when you settle down, marry, and have children? Is it over when you find your true calling in life and give your best effort to carry out your duties? Is it over when you have finished your task and can look back in gratitude for the many blessings you have received? I know that you know the answer as well as I do: that in fact the struggle of faith is never over in this life. As long as we wake up to face a new day, in whatever season of life we find ourselves, there is always room for growth. Final release from the struggle of faith does not come in this life; it comes only on that glorious day when death itself is swallowed up in victory. In whatever time of life we find ourselves, let us press on eagerly to the high prize of our calling (Philippians 3:14).

Brothers and sisters, the sin of Solomon is certainly a warning, but it is also a challenge. At the highest point of Israel's monarchy, the glory of God and the glory of a human kingdom touched. The human kingdom eventually passed away; but the glory of God has not. Well beyond the borders of ancient Israel, well beyond the lifetime of a single king, well beyond the very institution of monarchy, the glory of God in the rule of Christ extends over the whole of creation. It is not a rumor or a dream; it is a present reality, seen by all with the eyes of faith. Let us not only give him our best; let us go on giving, while life endures.

VI

PSALM 127

The Psalms contain a startling truth: human emotional life is not foreign to the living reality of almighty God. On the contrary, the intimate mysteries of emotional well-being are at the center of divine compassion for all human existence. Surely anyone who reads the Psalter is immediately overwhelmed by the astonishing range of human feeling that it expresses. Nothing human is removed from its concern. And yet the struggle throughout the Psalter is to understand the world of human feeling in the light of God's abiding presence. Our psalm for today is no exception; it seeks to open for us a window of fresh air in the life of Christian discipleship. Let us consider its witness. Brothers and sisters, hear the Word of God.

Psalm 127 is described as "a song of ascents of Solomon." Two comments are in order about this description, before we plunge into the text of the psalm itself. First, apparently the psalms entitled "song of ascents" or "song of degrees" were originally songs to be sung on pilgrimage to Jerusalem. They would have been sung by faithful Israelites on their way to the capitol city to observe the required festivals. But like all the psalms, these pilgrim psalms have been placed in the new context of the Bible's book of prayer. They were once songs for believers on a journey; but now they are the means through which God teaches every new generation the true way of obedience. Second, this psalm is associated with Solomon. Immediately the image of Israel's third king is conjured up before our eyes. How was Solomon to carry out the wide range of obligations that his sacred office had laid upon him? How was he to do his best as Israel's king? But once again, we must observe that the psalm, though associated with Solomon, is now sacred Scripture for the whole community of faith. It raises the question for every believer: How are the many duties of life to be accomplished?

We live in an incredible time in human history. Opportunities that were once reserved for the chosen few are now open to anyone who would pursue them. Goods and services that once were available to only a small percentage of humankind are now familiar features of everyday life for everyone. The glories of human culture, which could once be enjoyed only by a special clientele, are now available for everyone to treasure. If anything, the growth of technology seems only to aid in this general enrichment of the human community. But with this increase in the complexity of the world in which we live comes a basic question that every human being faces: What am I to do with all these new possibilities? How am I to spend the limited time that I have on this earth in the most appropriate way? Every human being faces these issues, and our psalm approaches them with total candor.

"Unless the LORD builds the house, those who build it labor in vain. Unless the LORD watches the city, the watchman stays awake in vain." The psalm begins with an unbreakable theological principle, which applies to every human being, in every conceivable situation. Despite the necessity of carrying out given duties, human labor does not build the house of God. God alone is the builder. God alone is responsible for every dimension of the life of his people, and he needs no help whatsoever in fulfilling his purposes. And again, despite the need for vigilance and care in watching over the community of faith, God alone protects and secures the lives of his people. He needs no help as Israel's defender. This principle immediately gives rise to a practical lesson for all human life. It is folly to force oneself to start on the duties of life at dawn, or to push oneself to keep on working long after the time to stop for the day has arrived. It is folly to force oneself to spend hours preparing a meal when simpler fare could be enjoyed by all. After all, who can enjoy what they have gained by working themselves to exhaustion? Despite the need to engage in the duties of life, the fact is that the gifts of God come to human beings, not when they are working, but when they are sleeping. It is a sheer illusion to ascribe bounty in life to work; for it is derived from one source only, and that is God.

The standard question of unbelief is always the same: What can I do to solve the problems of the world today? On the right, this question is framed in accordance with conservative values that guide human behavior; on the left, in the form of egalitarian ideals. But either way, the same results always obtain. First, the question expresses an obsessive restlessness, which consumes the joy of living that is at the heart of Christian faith. Second, in some cases so-called "problems" are solved that were never problems to begin with, spreading trouble and turmoil all around. And finally, time and energy are wasted, accomplishing nothing, with the simple result that essential duties are left undone. To approach life with that question is a complete contradiction of the true reality of Christian obedience. It may have an appearance of earnest intent; but in fact, it brings only harm to the church of Jesus Christ.

The right questions with which the Christian disciple approaches each new day are these: How can I give my very best to accomplish the tasks in life that I've been given to do? How can I obey the commandments of God to the very best of my ability? How can I strive for excellence in the service of Christ? We have all been given different tasks in life to carry out. Each one of them is absolutely crucial to the blessedness of God's kingdom. In this congregation, several fields of human endeavor are represented: business, education, agriculture, medicine, city government, the arts, and many more. God has not given you your duties in life in order to solve the problems of the world; that is his business, not yours. He has given you these duties as an incredible gift to be enjoyed to the very fullest extent possible. And the source of that joy is to give everything you have to carry them out. Work is not a burden; it is a liberation of every gift of human personality. Hold back nothing, and you will find total fulfillment in every labor.

The second part of the psalm makes what appears to be a radical shift in subject matter, but a closer inspection easily makes clear the connection. The psalm begins to speak about the joys of children. Human labor may foster the illusion that human beings provide for their own needs; but no one can be mistaken when it comes to the wondrous delight of children. They are truly a miracle of God. The birth of a child is brought about by God alone, who graciously gives a new life to be cherished by father and mother alike. There is no greater sense of purpose in life, no stronger support in times of difficulty, no more lasting source of comfort and enjoyment than one's children. Every burden in life can easily be borne by the one who knows how to relish time with children. Now the connection in subject matter is more clear; in sharp contrast to the fretful anxiety of the world's problem solver is the confident amazement of one who knows where true treasure in life is to be found: at home.

I scarcely need to tell this congregation what you already know so well. There is no greater thrill in life than the pride of a parent in the growth of a child. Who has not known intense and profound gratitude for every moment of a child's existence? Who has not felt the rush of excitement to see new adventures in learning, or new discoveries of hidden talent? Who would not gladly give up the wealth of the whole world to see one instant of a child's unrestrained glee, or to share even a single second of a child's ecstatic laughter? A child's speech is more tantalizing than the greatest novel ever written. No power in the universe compares to the potent magic of a child's grin. These pleasures are not added spices to the ordinary routines of daily living. These are the very purpose for which God put us on this planet. Joy in one's children is at the very center of life as God's creatures. It does not come and go with the seasons of life; it is an eternal gift, which only grows more extravagant and beautiful with time.

Brothers and sisters, I feel sure that all of us struggle with the concerns raised by this wise and powerful psalm. It is all too easy to slide into an attitude of unceasing worry, which does no good for us or for anyone else. But when we find ourselves facing such a temptation, the remedy is clearly before us. God does not want us to solve the world's problems, but he does want us to strive with all our might in doing life's tasks. And we do not need to look far afield to know where to find the greatest happiness in the universe. It is always closest to home. To work our hardest and to love with unbounded affection — a thousand lifetimes are not enough to hold the exquisite glories that these contain.

VII

FROM THE PARABLES

1. Matthew 25:14-30

We begin today a series of sermons based on several of the parables of Christ. Many of the parables of Jesus are among the best known and most treasured passages in the whole Bible. It is as if here, in the parables, the voice of Christ is heard in its most intimate immediacy. The canon of Scripture fixes the parables in their final form and thus insures a degree of continuity in their interpretation from one generation of the church to the next. Nevertheless, every age of the church has strained with all its might to catch every tone, lest a single note of rich beauty be overlooked. Moreover, it has long been the experience of faithful readers that the parables never cease to offer new perspectives of application to the daily Christian life. The voice of Christ at its most intimate is also at its most challenging. If we rightly discern the comparison to the kingdom of God that is being made by a parable, we cannot live the rest of our lives quite the same. Every parable changes forever the world of its reader. Today we begin with the parable of the talents. Brothers and sisters, hear the Word of God.

What is the kingdom of God like? A well-to-do man is preparing for a trip that will take him a long way from home. He knows he must give careful attention to his affairs before he leaves. He summons the servants who operate his household and divides among them control of his finances. He is fully aware of their varying capacities and appor-

81

tions the money appropriately: each servant receives more or less depending upon ability. The value of a talent varied in ancient times, but it was always high; so the financial stakes are considerable. Then he is off, a lengthy expedition ahead of him. As soon as he is gone, the servant who received the most cash puts it to work and doubles his stake. The next servant, who received somewhat less, accomplishes the same feat. But the third servant, who received the least amount, heads outside to dig a hole in the ground and buries the one talent he was given. The master of the household returns eventually and is ready to settle accounts with his servants. The first approaches him and tells him the generous profit that his money has earned. The master is effusive in his praise; he tells the servant what an excellent job he has done. He informs him that his fidelity and ingenuity in accomplishing the task assigned to him means that from now on far greater responsibility will be conferred upon him. The servant, though he is a subordinate of his master, is invited to join in the festive joy of new-found wealth. The second servant approaches his master with a similar account and receives in return a like response of beaming approval. The identical response of the master makes clear that the issue is not the exact amount made by each servant, but the degree of creative energy in handling the initial deposit.

Finally, the third servant comes to explain himself before his master. The contrast with the previous two could not be greater. Rather than using a tone of voice that is eager to please, he begins on the defensive and goes downhill from there. He lamely attempts to flatter his master in an effort to cover over his laziness, but the pathetic excuse he offers only makes matters worse. He tells his master that he knows how severe and exacting he is and that he is used to getting his way in all things regardless of the circumstances. So he decided to hide the talent rather than invest it, so as to be sure to have it safe and sound when the master returned. But the master sees right through this poor explanation for an even poorer performance. He blasts away at the indolence and insolence of his servant. If he was so sure that his master always gets what he wants, then at the very least he should have deposited the money in a bank for routine interest. As it is, the servant has shown himself to be useless. So the master directs that his money be taken from him and given to the one who has the most. The enterprising will

82

be given even more to work with, while the dull and lifeless will lose everything. The parable closes with the familiar New Testament idiom of final judgment, making clear that the censure of the worthless servant is an ultimate decision.

What does this parable mean for the way we live our lives in the modern world? First of all, it demands an active faith for the Christian. Of course, God is in control of the entire universe; God causes every event to occur, and nothing hinders his purpose. And yet there are no grounds whatsoever in Scripture for turning that biblical confession into a pretext for passivity in the Christian life. On the contrary, a passive faith is no faith at all. An active faith means that resources we have been given are not left to smolder, but are sought out enthusiastically and deployed effectively. An active faith means that risks are taken when the occasion requires it. It means that we recognize an opportunity in life when it is offered to us and drop everything else in order to make full use of it. An active faith gladly incurs short-term losses for the sake of long-term gains; it willingly abandons diversions for the supreme joy to be found in a focused effort; it looks to Christ alone as the final judge of human action and leaves to others the back and forth of human opinion. An active faith is the fullness of life.

Second, this parable makes clear the importance of using our intelligence, of thinking and acting for ourselves. There is nothing more sad in our times than the oppressive and predictable sameness of the party-line, whether on the left or on the right. A living faith never yields to pressure to stay in line with any human platform. The Christian is free to roam at will in exploring the many options of human endeavor in contemporary times. Scripture sets out a range of possibilities, and the Christian is encouraged to make the most of human culture in searching for the best one. Now, if we come up against a boundary-line of our faith, then we must never cross it. When Scripture says no, the answer is always no. But when Scripture says yes, it usually leaves an open field of wonderful possibilities to explore. The self-reliance of the Christian means that no strictures or prejudices of human ideology be allowed to restrain the full exuberance of life's thrills. Such thrills are given by God himself to expand the enjoyment of the Christian to the fullest extent; a timid faith misses the forest of delight for the trees of human bias.

Third, it is crucial to recognize the element of risk in genuine faith. Perhaps you have caught yourself asking on occasion: Am I doing the right thing? Am I really sure that I have moved the right direction in the decisions that I have made? No one likes uncertainty; it would be nice if you could see ahead far enough to be absolutely sure of the consequences of your actions. But you can't; the best that you can do is take the path in life that appears to you to be the most promising. If you meet with obstacles along the way, don't panic and decide that it is all a mistake; work around them one at a time and recognize that the trail moves ahead on the other side just as you had hoped. God does not expect you to see what lies at the end of all your efforts in life; he only expects that you travel forward in a spirit of adventure and conquer whatever fears would hold you back.

Finally, it is necessary to speak of the passion of faith. The passion of faith has nothing to do with revolutionary fanaticism. Fanaticism always gives out in the end; it turns whatever gain has been accomplished into a destructive menace; it tears down whatever progress of human welfare it has brought about, leaving suffering and misery in its wake; it turns against the people it would claim to help and becomes in fact their worst enemy. There is nothing fanatical about Christianity. And yet, a faith without passion is a contradiction in terms. The passion of faith knows how to distinguish the fads of clever packaging from the genuine truths that good men and women have lived and died for. The passion of faith wastes no time on grudges, or climbing the ladder of success, or manipulating people and events; it knows exactly what it wants, goes straight for it, and never lets go. The passion of faith is irrepressibly infectious, so it has no need to display itself. If it goes into a slump, it bounces right back with even greater force; if it hits a wall, it goes over or around it. It is relentless in its desire to make the most of life, and it struggles for triumph until life itself gives way. The passion of faith brings life to light in all the earth.

Brothers and sisters, the venture of faith changes the whole world of human experience. What was once scattered is now gathered; what was once confused is now clear; what was once a burden is now the greatest pleasure. Let us never be tempted to temper the daring boldness of faith by a false sense of pious obligation. Scripture tells us where our duties are absolutely binding in all circumstances; but it also releases us to the freedom of discovery in the open field of human living. Let nothing hold you back, and the world cannot contain the riches you will find.

2. Luke 17:7-10

We continue today our series of sermons on several of the parables of Christ. We began last week by remarking upon the incredible mixture of intimacy and intensity that characterizes the parables of Jesus. Every parable contains a new world of human experience, and we must struggle to find our way around in unfamiliar territory. As we observed, the parable of the talents insists upon qualities of passion, risk, and self-reliance, characteristics that are hard to come by in an age of ideological conformity. And yet there is no genuine faith without these qualities, and so the stakes are enormously high. Our text for today likewise runs against the grain of modern Christendom, in both its liberal and conservative manifestations. The parables do not interpret the world; they define a new age of human existence open to all who would rise to the challenge. Brothers and sisters, hear the Word of God.

Jesus tells a story that clarifies the true ordering of life in the kingdom of God. The story presupposes the institution of slavery, which thankfully has long ago been eliminated; so we must use our historical imagination to gather the insights contained in the story. Imagine a landowner with many servants. The landowner assigns his servants chores in the field, both planting the crops and tending the animals. They put in a good day's work and head home after everything is finished. When they arrive at the house, what happens? Does the master tell them: "Now that you've done your part serving me, it's my turn to serve you! Rest yourself, and I will bring you a hearty meal to enjoy!" No, that is not how it works between a master and a servant. Every listener in the ancient audience to which Christ was speaking knew the proper way things are done. When the servant returns from the day's work, he does not stop being a servant; rather, he continues his role by doing his part in preparing the meal and waiting upon his master. When the needs of his master are fully satisfied, only then does he see to his own. And the appropriate response of the master is not a fulsome expression of gratitude; a servant is a servant, and he earns no extra credit for doing what his position in life requires. The lesson for Christian discipleship is brought home by Jesus: when the servants of Christ have obeyed all the commandments they have been given to do, their response is simply to acknowledge the profound humility of their role in life in the performance of their obligations: "We are unworthy servants; we have only done what was our duty."

The parable that we are considering today, the parable of the unworthy servants, is a serious indictment of the modern Christian church. The modern church is built upon a question that is asked both on the theological left and on the theological right: How can the Christian gospel meet my needs? The question gets played out in a thousand different variations. How can the gospel secure my future? How can the gospel solve the problems of the world? How can the gospel guarantee a stable family life? How can the gospel erase all distinctions of class? And so on. Millions of dollars are spent every year to advertise the Christian faith on the basis of this question, in one of its forms. Pastors are trained to frame every sermon in accordance with the rules of discourse that this question fosters. Individual Christians are educated to see the world through the lens of the answers that are received. There is only one problem: the question is false, and the answers are worthless. However well-intended the search, this approach to the gospel leads to ruin for the church.

The gospel turns the world upside down. The cutting edge of the church's life is not yet another answer to these same tired questions, but a whole new question: What do I owe to Jesus Christ? I am not my own; I belong to him, body and soul. What does he want me to do with my life? Let us consider for a moment today the answer to this question.

First of all, your mind belongs to him. To serve Christ requires the rigorous application of the Christian's intelligence. It takes no thought whatsoever to accept the standard line of either conservative or liberal theology. We need only to subscribe to the party publication, read an article or two, and we know what to think. This is a sad parody of the intellectual adventure of Christian discipleship. Every passage of Scripture contains a truth ready to be learned afresh and applied. We have been given minds so that we can recognize and embrace those truths to the best of our ability, not so that we can smother them with ideological dogma. To obey Christ is to think for oneself and to feed the mind with resources to carry out its task to the fullest extent. A living faith is a mind awake.

Second, your body belongs to him. He did not put you in a body to be used for your convenience until it someday stops working for good. He made you a physical creature, with limits to observe and opportunities to cultivate. What happens if you ignore those limits? If you push yourself too hard, then you are giving away the rewards of daily life; you are giving away the joy of labor, the delights of food and drink, the unconscious stimulus of relaxation, the release of tension in exercise, the exalted beauty of family love. What opportunities are we given? The body ties us together with the rest of creation. Humankind alone is made in the image of God; yet humankind is a creature of the earth, united in the rhythms of nature with all other creatures. The advances of modern culture have largely closed off the access of humankind to the natural world in daily life, whether through the drowning of the night sky by the glare of big-city lights or through the erasure of close contact with plant and animal life through the destruction of natural habitats. But anyone who lives in a rural community has a wealth of possibility for the routine enjoyment of creation not available elsewhere, and we should not overlook the special blessings that brings.

Third, our emotional life belongs to him, both in a negative and in a positive sense. In the negative sense, if we know some item is beyond our means, there is no excuse for leaving it to the heart as a plaything for human avarice. If it is wrong to own it, then it is wrong to want to own it. Scripture speaks of the need for self-control, and it never commands what we are not able to obey. Whatever would entice us, even if we never act to acquire it, should be off-limits for the emotions as well. In the positive sense, you know best what is right for your life within the bounds set by Scripture. You can gather as much advice as you need, if that is what you want to do; but always trust your own instincts when it comes to questions of human happiness. If there is something you desire, go for it, and don't worry about what others think; if there is something you enjoy, make time in your life to draw from it the last ounce of pleasure; if there is something you dream, then be willing to pay any price to get it. A dream fulfilled erases from the memory even the slightest trace of regret and brings a wealth of excitement never even anticipated.

Fourth, your will belongs to him. Christian discipleship does not simply happen. It requires decisions, decisions that affect even intimate details about how we live our lives. Both conservative and liberal Christianity seek to remove from Christian practice the need for any decisions in life. Christian discipleship is presented to the followers of these ideologies as a package deal, with pre-established options depending on how much one wants to invest. Nothing could be further from the dazzling picture of daily Christian life presented in Scripture, which demands our whole being. Biblical freedom requires decisions. Decision making is not necessary unless we're uncertain about the best way to go. Christian existence involves bold decisions that directly affect the way we spend our time and talents. No one can tell us in advance that we have made the right decision. We have to try it out for ourselves and see where it leads. But once you have made the decisions you must make, don't let anyone or anything shake your self-confidence. Decide with daring, then be filled with calm, knowing that you have done your best. All the comforts of divine care are hidden in the gamble of a good choice.

Brothers and sisters, the world right side up is the world in which we are servants of Jesus Christ. The traditional liturgy of the church contains a beautiful phrase: "the service of Christ is perfect freedom." The wisdom of a hundred generations of Christians is contained in this single saying. For we do not find that obeying Christ suppresses our humanity; just the opposite is the case. Christians the world over have long known that doing God's will energizes human personality to the greatest degree possible. The gospel teaches us how to think with a God-given mind that is ready for action; how to move around in the glory of creation with eyes wide open and hands eager to touch; how to magnify the fullness of what we have, not brood over what we don't have; how to triumph in the decisions that life brings along, never once looking back. The new world of Christian discipleship is a new creation of authentic humanity.

3. Matthew 18:21-35

We continue today our series of sermons on the parables of Christ. Each parable is a new world of human discovery. We can try our best to fit it in with patterns of behavior with which we are already familiar and comfortable; yet in doing so we may lose the opportunity for insight and growth that is extended to us. Or we can take a chance that what is contained in the parables is worth throwing away our preconceived ideas; then we find that the new world of God's kingdom is more wonderful than we could ever imagine. We did not expect even a fraction of what we find. Last week we reflected upon the parable of the unworthy servants and the comprehensive obligations implied in our service to Christ. We noted the paradox that we owe him our whole being, yet what we receive in return is the fullest abundance of living. Our parable for today uncovers the genuine quality of mercy that is necessary for disciples of Christ. Brothers and sisters, hear the Word of God.

The apostle Peter puts to Jesus the question that gives rise to the parable of the unforgiving servant. There is no reason to doubt the honesty of Peter's intentions; he simply wants to know where the limits of human compassion are located for the followers of Christ. How many times should I overlook the faults of others? Are there narrow limits or broad limits to forgiveness? As often happens in discussions with Christ in the Gospels, he does not answer the question as it is posed to him. The force of Christ's response is not to say, well, yes, there are broad limits. The point, rather, is that there are no limits at all; the question is false, because it presupposes a conception of human mercy that is foreign to the divine expectation for human life. The parable of the unmerciful servant is not therefore intended to reinforce a point that Peter can easily grasp. Instead, it is meant to teach what is clearly beyond any conception that Peter has ever entertained.

The rule of God in human life is comparable to a king who decides it is time to settle financial accounts with his servants. It is not long before a servant appears who owes him an outrageous sum of money. The size of the debt is colossal, and yet the resources of the servant are nonexistent. The only source of income he has is his own person and the persons of his wife and children. At a time when human slavery was

89

acceptable, the sale of human beings into servitude would be the last resort when all other expedients had failed. The king makes the natural decision: the servant and his family are to be sold as slaves, and the profit earned is to be used to pay off the huge debt. But the servant falls down prostrate before the ruler and begs for mercy. He asks to be given time to pay off the debt. The ruler sees before him a man pleading for his own life and the lives of his family, and he is overcome with pity. He not only grants the man's request for patience; he goes even further and simply cancels the loan outright. The man and his family are free to go, unburdened by any further obligation.

The story follows the same servant as he leaves the presence of the king. He finds another servant, who happens to owe him money, a trifling pittance compared to the fortune of debt from which he has just been released. He grabs the second servant by the throat and angrily demands: "Pay me what you owe!" The second servant falls to his knees, just as the first had before the king. He makes the same appeal for clemency and promises to pay everything back in due course. The first servant not only fails to extend the forgiveness he had received; he is even unwilling to accept a grace period for repayment. He automatically applies the harshest measures: the man is cast into debtor's prison until full recovery of the tiny amount is extracted. Now, other servants see all these events as they unfold, and they are extremely upset. They go to the king and give a detailed report of the first servant's actions. The servant is summoned back before the king, who bitterly reprimands him. What he has done is inexcusable; his own massive debt has been canceled, simply because he asked for forbearance. Can he not see that he therefore owes the same degree of tolerance that he has received? The king is livid, and he hands the hard-hearted servant over to the jailers, whose job it is to squeeze out of him every last penny they can find. The message of the parable is brought home for the disciples of Christ: God will treat with like severity any who do not behave toward others with spontaneous kindness and mercy.

What does this parable teach us about the Christian life in our time and place? The first point is a crucial one: all Christian ethics are grounded in theology. The way we treat others is based upon the way we are treated by God himself. What is the gospel message? The gospel does not say that God gives us a second chance in life. It does not say,

"You have wasted all these years abusing the gifts you've been given, and violating the commandments you have received, but don't worry, you now have time to make up for lost ground." No, instead the gospel says: "The past is the past. Leave it in the past where it belongs. Start afresh on the road to freedom." The Christian faith offers a new beginning of service to God, which is always focused upon the future. God does not expect a return on the sins of the past; he gives what he gives free of charge, and his gifts are the best joys of human existence.

And now we come to the second point. It is simply not an option for Christians to withhold from others the astonishing gift of compassion that we have received from God himself. Here a chief culprit is the harboring of grudges. To harbor a grudge means to fix in the memory every small act of unkindness that we have received from others, whether real or imagined. To harbor a grudge is to carry in the mind an exact ledger of the misdeeds of others toward us. At best, it is to wait until we receive a *quid pro quo,* an act of goodness that in our opinion wipes the slate clean. At worst, it means a permanent lowering of the status of others in our own estimation, based upon the strenuous mathematics of moral judgment. In any case, it is a habit of mind and relationship to others that must be identified and rooted out. No one likes to be on the receiving end of a slight, or an insult, or an outright personal affront. Yet how many times have we let slip words or deeds that we later regretted? Our job in life is to treat every other person with the greatest amount of respect and affection that we know how to give. If someone falters, let it go, and look for a fresh opportunity to deepen a friendship; life is too short to waste even one hour in bitterness.

A third point is more positive in its orientation. As Christians, it is our duty to live life full of affirmation of human excellence in all its infinite variety. There is no one prototype of an ideal personality, with ideal gifts; and if we approach reality with such a prototype in mind we will lose our appreciation for the resplendent vitality of the human community. Each new generation brings a wave of fresh voices of leadership in the church. If we compare these voices with an echo from the distant past, we will never hear what they have to say. Instead, we should listen as if we are hearing the message that they bring for the first time. The canon of Scripture establishes a range of legitimate possibilities for Christian proclamation. Every age of the church has the responsibility to determine, through experimentation and analysis, what combination of sounds to produce. If new harmonies are formed, that is not a loss for the church but a gain; if new insights are won, that is not a criticism of the church but a challenge; if new joys are felt, that is not a restriction but an invitation.

Brothers and sisters, the Christian faith does not skim across the surface of human existence; it reaches down to where we live our lives in daily experience. It does not merely help us to understand the frailties of human psychology; it tells us what pleases God and what is totally unacceptable to him. As followers of Jesus Christ, we must walk away from resentment and envy of others. We are not asked to become more liberal in our assessment of the motives of others; we are told by the gospel that we cannot possibly know what those motives are, and hence we have no right whatsoever to base our response upon our own ignorant projections. If we think we know why others do what they do, we are wrong; if we act upon what we think, we are doubly wrong. But if we leave all judgment to God, we are right; and if we treat others with the same infinite kindness we have received, we obey the commandment of Christ. The glory of heaven above shines on all our deeds.

4. Matthew 13:44

We continue today our series of sermons based upon the parables of Christ. The teaching of Christ encapsulated in the parables clearly stands in the great prophetic tradition of Israel's Scripture. The kingdom of God impinges directly upon human existence, and humankind stands exposed before the penetrating reality of divine judgment. All that is trivial is swept aside by the life-or-death decisions required by the encroaching rule of God. And yet the preaching of Christ flashes with a brilliance of human pleasure that is unique. Of all the parts of the Christian canon, the purest tone of absolute joy is heard most clearly in the parables of Jesus. When it sounds, anyone with ears to hear is overcome by its unmistakable wonder. Brothers and sisters, hear the Word of God.

Somewhere hidden in the earth there is a fortune. We do not know how it got there. Was it left accidently? Was it buried in the forgotten past and left undetected for generations? Did its owner pass away before being able to retrieve it? We do not know. What we do know is that it is somewhere out in the countryside and that it is carefully concealed from human sight, until one day, when a man happens to find it. Again, we do not know what brought him there. Had he heard rumors of buried treasure? Was he looking for something that he had lost? Was he going about routine business, when the merest chance altered his luck forever? We do not know. But we do know that the man plays it smart right from the very beginning of his incredible find. He doesn't claim the fortune for himself right away; after all, there is clearly the chance of a legal claim by whoever owns the field. Nor does he advertise his prize; we can only imagine how hard it was to keep quiet about such an amazing event. Instead, he makes sure that the treasure remains completely out of sight. He finds out how much the field would cost. Despite the fact that he cannot afford it, he realizes that this is a once in a lifetime opportunity that only a fool would pass up. He knows that something inexpressibly grand has entered his life, and he can scarcely contain his exuberance. So he sells everything he owns in order to buy that field. And suddenly, he is rich beyond all ordinary comprehension. He is set for life.

What are the true marks of genuine Christian faith? To begin with, the Christian always takes the initiative. The Christian does not wait until the times come along and confirm in advance the proper direction in life to take. The Christian does what is right because it is commanded by God, not because that course is widely recognized by others. And what is the result of that initiative? The Christian is privileged to witness miracles of human happiness unspoiled by the piercing gaze of crowds. The Christian is lucky enough to share in the excitement of exploration, not following a map but creating a new one for others. The Christian engages in exercises of human creativity that transform given materials into whole new possibilities. The Christian achieves what was hitherto considered impossible, understands the answers to questions that are elsewhere not yet even asked, stands in awe of the mystery of life that is concealed from the inspection of curious bystanders. Never be afraid to seize the initiative, when you see in front of you a wonderful opportunity from God. Don't wait to see if others notice it too, or you may lose your opportunity.

We must also speak of the wisdom of faith. The Christian should never fall into the trap of acting without a clear understanding of cause and effect. We live in a time when the highest praises are heaped upon the unexamined expression of human desire. Great emphasis is placed on self-expression, on saying and doing whatever we want. We are constantly urged to "Just do it!" The problem with such advice is that it ignores the subtle rhythms of the universe in which we live. There is a time to speak; but there is also a time to keep our mouth tightly closed until it is proper to open it. There is a time to act; but there is also a time to keep our heads down and our footsteps steady. The illusion is that if we speak and act without self-restraint we will get whatever we want. The reality is that, without self-control, we only get what is second-best to begin with, and we soon lose even what we have. Take account of the distance between the effect you want and the cause that will bring it about. Take the time to travel that distance, and nothing can stop you from the enjoyment you seek.

Furthermore, it is important to recognize the solitude of faith. There is no question that the community life we share with others brings every blessing of comfort, thrill, and companionship that life affords. Human beings are social creatures, put by God himself into the company of others for our greatest good. The changing seasons of human experience enhance at every turn the unspeakable goodness of human fellowship. Still, it is one thing to recognize and appreciate fully the lifelong benefit of relationship to others. It is quite another to lose ourselves in the mass of human society. Christian faith upholds the integrity of the individual. How can we give to others, if we do not take the time to replenish our resources? How can we provide for others, if we do not labor in the fields of human endeavor? How can we see ahead, if our eyes are not free to scout out the terrain over which we travel? How can we observe what we see, unless our minds are accustomed to picking out the familiar shapes and sounds of the objects around us? Do not be afraid to spend time alone in the doing of God's will. What you bring to the rest of the community will not suffer; on the contrary, you will have far more to give for the untold riches that you acquire.

Moreover, we must also speak of the unreserved determination of faith. Our culture knows how to applaud a good effort. It tells us: "If something is worth having only a little, then give only a little; but if it is worth having a lot, be willing to give a lot." That is true enough as far as it goes. Yet it does not take into account those decisions in life which require that we give everything we have, holding nothing back in reserve. Faith never shies away from such decisions. In fact, it quickly recognizes that those are precisely the decisions that draw us closer to the living reality of God. In faith, we must put our personal comfort on the line; we inherit in return a hiding place of divine compassion in which we will flourish beyond adequate description. In faith, we must yield up our carefully laid plans; we reap in return an eternal divine purpose of education and accomplishment. In faith, we must relinquish the visible role of leading the pack; we undertake in return the invisible role of charting the future. When it comes to the kingdom of God, giving a little is useless; giving a lot is not enough. Put your entire existence into play and see how stunning the results will be.

Then, too, we must speak of the focus of faith. The Christian life does not unfold in short bursts of energy that reappear now and then as the occasion demands. There is certainly an ebb and flow, periods of intense effort followed by exalted rest. But seen as it were from above, the characteristic track of the Christian life is the straight line that it leaves behind. Once again, Christian existence moves against the current of modern culture. The purpose of work, we are told, is to supply purchasing power for as many distractions as we can afford. The happiest person is the one who is distracted the most. But here, the Christian knows better. We all appreciate the breaks in routine that come our way, whether a family vacation, a night out on the town, or a special treat. Yet we do not live to be distracted; we live because God has filled the patterns of everyday life with infinite wealth. Money cannot buy the pride of a parent in the growth of a child; human resources can never manufacture the smiling face of a friend; no award can match the glory of a goal in life achieved after sustained effort over time. Look for tremendous fun in distractions; look for satisfaction beyond fulfillment in the simple gifts of living.

Brothers and sisters, there is no greater joy in all the earth than the service of Jesus Christ. That service may cost us everything we have; but it gives us in return a new world of triumphant celebration. It will cost us our time, but it will give us back the transcendent fullness of life. It will cost us our relationships, but it will give us back the sweetest loves ever known to humankind. It will cost us our pursuits in life, but it will give us back the highest goals of human achievement. It will cost us our self-will, but it will give us back the glory of freedom. Is it worth it? All the saints of all times agree: yes, it is well worth it.

5. Luke 18:1-8

We conclude today our series of sermons based upon the parables of Christ. The reading of Scripture requires a subtle understanding of the role of human imagination. On the one hand, we obviously bring to the text of the Bible our own experience in life. It is our duty to acquire and to perfect the resources that we bring, in the hope that every nuance of Scripture will become clear. Yet on the other hand, the goal of interpretation is not at all to fit the Bible into the world of our experience. Such an effort would gain nothing and lose everything. Rather, the goal is to move from the witness of the text to the reality of which it speaks. Every human preconception must be abandoned; every canon of human logic must be suspended; every human agenda must be set aside once and for all. The effort required to move from the text to the reality will cost us everything that we have to offer. But if we will pay that price, we will no longer be looking into a mirror of our own inner reflection; we will be gazing into the face of the living God. Brothers and sisters, hear the Word of God.

The parable of the unjust judge begins with a brief statement of purpose. Every disciple faces the ongoing temptation of fatigue and despair. Every follower of Christ knows those moments when all resources have been expended, and the only decision left seems to be to throw in the towel. In particular, the disciple is tempted by trials in life to cease calling upon God for help. Yet the disciple must never give in to the drain of weariness upon the life of faith. Jesus tells a story: There was once a judge who had no conscience whatsoever. He had no religious convictions, and he was completely devoid of sympathy for his fellow human beings. One day this judge is approached by a widow, the person least protected by legal rights in ancient times. She is in his jurisdiction, and she brings before him a case involving a dispute between herself and an opponent. She asks the judge to give her justice against her enemy. At first, the judge does exactly what one would expect: he ignores this insignificant claim upon his time and attention. But the woman won't go away; she comes back again and again, making the same request for vindication. Finally, the judge changes his mind and rules in her behalf — not because he gives a hoot about her predicament or because he thinks it is the right thing to do, but simply because he does not want to get worn out telling her no. "She is causing too much trouble and may do me in." Christ tells his listeners that the reason the judge gives for his change of heart is the key to the parable. Then he explains his point: If a wicked judge is moved to compassionate action by an evil motive, how much more will God act on behalf of his own, whom he has freely chosen to love? Will he delay long over them? No, he will quickly right the wrongs that they face, and he will answer their prayers with swift response. Nevertheless, Jesus concludes, despite the direct intervention of God in human existence, it remains an open question whether any genuine faith will greet the return of Christ at the close of the age.

The truth of the parable of the unjust judge, as radiant as it is in its own right, is magnified into infinity by the fact that God is not an unjust judge. God made the heavens and the earth to stand in independence from himself. God is self-contained, and he is not moved by any necessity to enter into relationship with what he has made. It is not need that binds God to humankind; it is the freedom of authentic love. God does not love because he has to in order to be God. Such a love would stem from divine weakness and would be of no benefit to humanity whatsoever. God loves his creatures because he wants to, in the sovereign decision of his eternal purpose. To provide for our needs does not diminish his resources; he made the universe to serve our welfare in life. To look after our good is not a limitation of his time; he entered human space and time for our redemption, and he made the seasons of life for human happiness. To see to the details of our concerns is not too minute for his attention; he was once wrapped in swaddling clothes to block out the cold night air, and he knows firsthand the sting of the lash on human skin. Not because he needs to, but because he wants to, God in Christ has made the intricate dimensions of our experience more familiar to himself than they are to us, so that he can guide us to their fullest expression of pleasure.

The realization of God's care changes forever the way we live our lives. We must first of all speak of the buoyancy of faith. As Christians we are obligated to give our very best effort to every duty in life that God has given to us. Some may disagree with the way we spend our time; others may disagree with the way we use our talents and energies. But at the end of the day, we will not face the court of human opinion. We will appear before the figure of Christ, whose servants we are, and there receive the only reckoning that really matters. How does this affect our daily existence? Whether intended or not, insults swirl around every one of us in the decisions of life. There is a certain pluck to faith that simply refuses to waste any time chasing down the good opinion of others. Any time we spend warding off an insult is time we could have used to give depth and perspective to our skills and labors. Don't cave in at the least hint of human disapproval; remember whom you serve, stay on course, and let events unfold as they will.

We must also speak of the serene tenacity of faith. Once we make the decision of faith, there is no looking back. It is astonishing how clearly the path emerges before us in the pursuit of God's kingdom. We see where we are headed, even if from a distance, and the turmoil and agitation that surround us suddenly fade into the background. How can we ever again wander away from the path in life that God shows us, once we see what lies at the other end? How could we ever settle for a short-cut, or an alternate route, when we have the assurance of God that our path is the only right one? How can we ever again be bothered by the boasts of others who claim to have seen a spectacular sideshow, when there in front of our very eyes is the boundless beauty of God's eternal realm? When you see where you are going in life, don't ever be talked out of following the path to the very end. The path itself is fantastic beyond human dreams; but what lies at the end of the path contains the wondrous joy that no human being can adequately express.

Third, we must speak of the unchanging role of prayer in the Christian life. Scripture knows very well of changing times in the cycles of human experience. What may apply at one age is no longer pertinent to another; what may attract and fulfill in one period of life may be a forgotten legacy in another. Christian faith enhances the unfolding of life in every stage. But certain aspects of discipleship are required at every age, and the chief of these is prayer. Every Christian, of every age, is summoned into the presence of God to pray. In fact, prayer is the life-long remedy against the threat of weariness. Prayer is a constant reminder that there is no substitute for doing the will of God. Prayer reminds us that the characteristic attitude of the Christian is the sparkle of human joy that pervades the whole person in all circumstances. Prayer points us, time and again, to the one source of all time and energy and the true measure of all human goodness, which is Christ. Prayer dissolves human troubles into the realization that we are not the only ones to suffer difficulties in life: not by a long shot are we the first generation of Christians to face an uphill struggle; not in the least are we the only Christians ever to pay a price for our faith. But no sooner do we enter into the joyful presence of God than the light of life illumines all reality with comfort and assurance. Never stop praying, until the God of life to whom you pray comes to take you to himself forever. Ask, and you will receive.

Brothers and sisters, it is impossible to summarize satisfactorily the lengths to which God goes in providing for our needs in life. Space does not constrict him; he owns the universe and guides all of humankind for our advantage. Time does not delay him; he captures the glory of the past for our instruction and prepares the elements of the future for our enrichment. He is not embarrassed by the mundane affairs of daily life; he once became a human being, turned water into wine to enhance the good cheer of human company, and cooked fish and bread to satisfy the hunger of his disciples. He is pleased when we believe that he wills our good in life, and when we act on the basis of that belief. There is no higher calling, and no finer delight, than to give pleasure to God by what we do in life. Who cannot see that it is our only duty, and our surest hope?

VIII

PSALM 30

The Psalms are insistent that every truth of God's Word is rightly perceived only in the context of human experience. One way in which they carry through this point is to assign titles to various psalms. The title given to our psalm for today in the King James Version is this: "A Psalm and Song at the dedication of the house of David." By setting this psalm within the life history of a single individual, the title directs the reader to a proper understanding of its message. Do we want to understand the subtleties of God's way in human life? Then we must observe God's work in the life of his servant David and the range of emotion that work evokes in David. Only then can we learn to harness our own emotional life to the living will of God. Let us consider today the witness of the thirtieth psalm. Brothers and sisters, hear the Word of God.

The first and second books of Samuel recount the life of David, which provides the initial clue for understanding the psalm. The road to the throne for David could hardly have been a more rocky one. He has been chosen by God from a large family much older and more accomplished than he. The only training he could bring to the task of ruling a kingdom was his instruction in the duties of a simple shepherd. And yet, one by one, every obstacle to his accession to the throne has been overcome. He has destroyed the giant Goliath in hand-to-hand combat. He has escaped the murderous rage of King Saul, who has become his own worst enemy and lapsed into self-destruction. He has united a divided kingdom, and the opposition has collapsed. Now the

Philistines are held in check, and the ark of the covenant has been re-stored to its rightful place in the Tabernacle. For the first time since the whole adventure began, David finds rest. He spends the first hours of peace in the new house that he occupies in the city of Jerusalem. Psalm 30 records this moment and the emotional struggle that led up to it.

To begin with, David knows exactly where to turn to give the credit for his triumph in life. His every thought is of God and the overwhelm-ing gratitude he feels toward the divine kindness. He expresses his ex-hilaration at the astonishing course covered by the last few years. God has brought him up out of hopeless circumstances and has entirely transformed the basic situation of his life. He has moved from the worst of times to the best of times. The loud boasting of his personal enemies has been silenced forever by the new direction in life God has bestowed upon him. David takes a moment to remember: there was a time when no future horizon appeared before his eyes, and every con-ceivable dimension of his life was out of joint. Without a single claim upon the divine aid, David simply asked for help in an impossible situ-ation. God put David's life back together again, piece by piece, until nothing but wholeness remained. The alteration was as great as a trans-formation from death to life. David's life was over, finished; but God hung on even when David couldn't, and, over time, brought him to the exalted place where he now celebrates life in supreme joy.

It is God who sets the goals for our lives, and he sets them far be-yond our own feeble imagination. Much of the time those goals seem simply unreachable. How can we beat the odds and achieve the unat-tainable? How can we pursue a straight course, when the winds blow so strongly from every direction? How can we go where others have not gone, if there are no markings to indicate our path? How can we endure the necessary hardships when our own makeup is so fragile? How can we accomplish a task that no one else agrees is doable? But at other times we reach a point in our lives when we begin to see, not only the uncertain road ahead, but also the path we have already covered. And the shock of recognition opens our eyes to the wonders of God's love. The trail has not meandered aimlessly through empty wasteland; it has moved from one point to another, along a clear line of progress through expansive and beautiful terrain. Every hardship has brought a fresh lesson in life that showed us the next step in our journey. Our abilities have been miraculously stretched by the challenges we have faced. We have discovered an inner strength that we never knew we had. We look around and realize that we are at the exact place, in the perfect time, doing the very thing that fulfills every dream we ever had. We are at home in the doing of God's will. And we owe everything we have to the luxury of God's grace.

The psalm continues by instructing the faithful concerning their obligation to render praise unto God for his bounty. They not only owe him everything that they have; they owe him a response of thanksgiving expressed in the communal liturgy of Israel's life. Their memories of his particular goodness to them are to be brought into the divine presence in worship. God's anger lasts only a moment, but his favor lasts a lifetime. The sting of God's judgment may at times provoke a sleepless night; but a ringing cry of exultant joy greets the dawn of a new day. The psalmist admits where he has gone wrong: when times were good, he thought he could relax his self-discipline. He thought he could throw off all self-restraint and never pay a price. He had momentarily forgotten the essential lesson that his whole life has taught him from the day of his birth: that strength is a divine gift, and not a human achievement. Just for a moment, God concealed his loving face from the psalmist, which threw him into deep despair. Already the psalmist has learned his lesson; he knows where to turn for help. He asks what good it will do if his life is allowed to be overthrown, for who will then praise God or witness to God's truth? He rests his case with God, not on any claim of merit to the divine attention, but on the forgiving disposition of God, who stands ever ready to lift up a faltering human being.

The opening section of the psalm captures the direction of a whole lifetime in the divine blessing; the next section, by contrast, shows the intermittent struggles that every Christian must face. No sooner do we see the goal that God would set for us than we strike out on our own to reach it the way we think best. God may set goals, we reason, but the path in life he leaves up to us. Human arrogance marks a direction in the blank landscape that lies before us, and we charge ahead without a second thought. But God will have none of it; he alone knows our path, and he will not accompany us on a wild goose chase. Usually we realize soon enough that we are on our own, lost, without comfort or provisions. Our only hope is to ask God to show us where we have gone wrong and to return us to the proper path. He never fails to answer that prayer. Terror gives way to certainty; anxiety gives way to assurance; inner turmoil gives way to perfect peace. God alone is the true pathmaker in life. He not only wants our best; he alone knows the only way to reach it, in the doing of his commandments.

The psalm returns once again to the present moment of sheer exhilaration, which finds David in rapturous ecstasy in the new palace. God has directly intervened in his life for the good. It is not simply a question of bringing a period of suffering to an end. Rather, God has taken away the most profound sorrow a human being can endure and put in its place absolute joy. God has removed the slightest traces of grief and left nothing but utter delight. The psalm concludes with a clear statement of the change that has taken place. The purpose of God's act of kindness is to create a space for David to join in the chorus of praise to God and not be reduced to sheer silence. So David makes the pledge that will henceforth guide his whole existence: forevermore, he will bring to God the song of gratitude that rightfully belongs to him.

Brothers and sisters, the character in this psalm is not a vile sinner or a worthless fool. The one whose experience is a guide to our own is King David, a "man after God's own heart." There is not a hint in this psalm of bad faith or evil intentions; David has made mistakes, and it is crucial for him to acknowledge this, but they are the mistakes of a saint and not a sinner. No one here today can deny that we have all made these same mistakes often enough. We have all assumed at one time or another that we know better than God does how to use the gifts he has given us and how to reach the goals he has set for us. When God corrects our false assumptions, it is not in order to crush us; it is because he values the contribution we make even more than we do ourselves. He has put us on this earth to bear witness to his goodness by what we say and do. Let us resolve this day to pursue that end until the day we die.

IX

FROM THE LIFE OF ELIJAH

1. 1 Kings 17

We begin today a series of sermons based on the figure of Elijah. The stories of the prophet Elijah are contained in the second half of the book of 1 Kings. We will, over the next few weeks, look at a series of episodes from his life; each episode draws out a different dimension of his ministry. Elijah's life and ministry take place during the twenty-two-year reign of King Ahab over Israel. The text of Scripture is frank: Ahab is the worst king who ever ruled over God's people. He not only continues the sad legacy of disobedience already well entrenched in Israel's monarchical tradition; he goes well beyond his predecessors in flagrantly violating the divine command. He is egged on by his wife Jezebel, daughter of a Sidonian king, who entices him into the idolatrous worship of Baal. Ahab builds a temple for Baal in Samaria and institutes public worship of Baal. Israel's very existence is at stake in confronting this threat, and it falls to the prophet Elijah to deliver the message of divine warning. He does so with unforgettable drama. Brothers and sisters, hear the Word of God.

As with other characters in the Bible, the Scriptural account of Elijah shows no interest in abstract biographical details. It merely mentions his origins in the remote province of Gilead, east of the Jordan River. What matters is his call and the office that he executes. Elijah is a prophet of God, commissioned by God to declare his will to the people of Israel. His entry onto the scene of world history could not possibly be more intense or more decisive. He tells King Ahab that a period of unprecedented drought will immediately befall the kingdom. Not a drop of rain will fall until Elijah declares otherwise. During this time of national disaster, Elijah himself is commanded by God to go into hiding by a small stream that feeds into the Jordan River. The stream is on Elijah's home turf in Gilead. He is told by God that he will have plenty to drink from the stream and that the birds will provide for all his needs for food. Elijah obeys, and he is taken care of for a time exactly as God had stated. But after a while, the effects of the drought reach directly into the personal life of Elijah himself. The stream dries up, with no run-off to fill it. Once again, God directs him to a place of safety, this time beyond the border of Israel to the north, in the Sidonian town of Zarephath. There, a certain poor widow is waiting to see to his needs.

The sweep of God's care for human life is incalculably rich and awesome in its mystery. God rules the entirety of human history in every detail. We are not prophets, and so we do not know the future as Elijah did. But we do know that every event that occurs transpires at the sovereign direction of God. Now, it would be easy to be led from this truth into a general theory of divine causality. God causes everything, and so every individual is but a pawn in a divine chess game. But it is just here that Scripture contains such a surprising and wondrous witness. For the testimony of Scripture is that God lavishes his special attention upon the lives of individual Christians. Individuals are not fitted into the patchwork of history. It is just the reverse: God himself marshals all the resources of human history to sustain and nourish the life of the individual.

What does this mean for your own relationship to God? Every day on the evening news, or as you read the newspaper, you witness human events that clearly effect your own life. You do not live in a historical vacuum, and even Christians must await with the rest of the world the ongoing development of human affairs. But the action of God in your own life is not limited to the general flow of the times in which you live. The God who governs all time applies his unlimited resources to your individual welfare and pleasure. If the times are rushed, he preserves for you a place to grow at your own pace. If circumstances are constrained, he brings before you a wide open space to enjoy and to explore to your heart's content. If the possibilities of one option in life are exhausted, he ushers you forth to a whole new world of human experience that he has already prepared — a world that contains not only what you lost, but more than you could ever anticipate. God controls history; but he does not fit you into history. Instead, he uses history to transport into your life every possible blessing.

Once again, Elijah obeys the divine summons. He makes the long journey from Gilead to Sidon and eventually arrives at the coastal town of Zarephath. As soon as he arrives, he encounters the woman with whom his own life is now to be so closely tied. She is by the gate of the city, gathering bits of kindling for a fire. He acts upon the basis of the divine promise and begins telling her what he needs: a drink of water and something to eat. She starts out for the water, but when she hears the request for bread she expresses her dismay. She and her son are at the very end of their provisions. The flour in the jar is almost gone, and the jug of oil is all but empty. In fact, she tells him, her intentions were to gather wood for one last fire, to make one last meal before she and her son would die. But Elijah brings her news that changes her life forever. He tells her to do as she planned, bringing him a cake of bread and then one each for her and her son. For God will never allow the flour or oil to run out until the drought is ended. She does what he tells her, and they have plenty to eat from then on.

The ways of God in human life are as unexpected as they are majestic. Here in Gilead is a man with the promise of God, needing food and drink; there, in a different country, is a widow with a son to care for, at her wits' end. And yet, in an instant their lives are bound together under the eternal protection of God. It is easy to understand if we struggle with moments of doubt or reluctance. But it is important not to dwell on these struggles but to put them behind us as quickly as they arise. The clear path of Christian obedience is to embrace with eager affirmation the opportunities for service of Christ that God opens up in front of our eyes. Such opportunities will meet every need that we have, and many that we are not even aware of. They will result in inexhaustible benefit for countless numbers of people. Looking ahead, the plan of God may be uncertain, and at times difficult to discern; but looking back, it is always clear that God acted at the right time, and in the right way, to give us the deepest satisfaction of our every desire in life.

From the Life of Elijah

After a time, a crisis hits close to home in the life of Elijah and his adopted family. The widow's son falls gravely ill and stops breathing. The woman understandably panics and blames Elijah for her son's death. She accosts him with bewildered agony: "Why have you come here, you prophet, just to remind me of my sins and to take away my dearest possession?" Elijah gently ignores the insult and instead takes direct action on her behalf. He tells the woman to give him her son and reaches to gather him from her anguished grasp. He takes the child with him up to his room in the attic and lays him out upon the couch where he sleeps. He addresses God with his own heartfelt prayer of distress: "Has your anger over Israel's sins even come to this kindly woman, who has so diligently cared for my needs?" He covers the child with his own body and three times asks God to restore his life. And God answers his prayer. Elijah brings the child with him down into the house and gives him back to his mother. In simple words that contain a world of relief, exhilaration, and utter amazement, he tells her: "Look here, your boy is healthy again." She wastes no time in apologizing: she tells him that from now on she is absolutely certain of his unique calling from God.

Brothers and sisters, God not only wants the very best for our lives. He also wants us to know for sure from whom we have received the precious gifts we enjoy. Every single facet of the good life that is ours comes directly from God's own hand. There are times for all of us when suffering temporarily interrupts the flow of blessing. None of us enjoys such suffering, and we would all rather do without it if we could. But the fact is that God himself brings it into our lives. Why? Has he suddenly decided he hates us after all? Has he suddenly concluded that we are not worth the effort? Not at all; quite the opposite. He reminds us, through our suffering, that the whole of life, in every detail, is laid out before us for our pleasure by him. Suffering is not the absence of God; it is the means by which he draws us closer to his presence. The shadow of suffering only serves to highlight the light of life, which illuminates nothing less than the whole of creation.

2. 1 Kings 18:17-46

We continue today our series of sermons on the prophet Elijah. Last week we considered the call of Elijah and the extraordinary announcement of drought that he was given by God to deliver to Israel. We observed the extent of the divine protection in guarding Elijah from harm and in providing for his comfort. We heard of the incredible miracle of healing with which God blessed the son of the widow who looked after Elijah's needs. We reflected upon the astonishing attention the Almighty God gives to the individual, even in difficult circumstances. In our text for today, three years have gone by, and God commands Elijah to return to King Ahab, to tell him that the drought is finally over. The stubbornness and arrogance of Ahab guarantee that even this good news cannot come without a confrontation. But Elijah is fully prepared for the task. Brothers and sisters, hear the Word of God.

Elijah comes to Ahab, but it is Ahab who immediately goes on the offensive. "Look who's here, the one making all the trouble for Israel." Elijah does not flinch; instead, he states the simple truth: that Ahab's disobedience to the divine commandments is the cause of all the harm that has descended upon God's people. Above all, Ahab has committed idolatry, which is a direct violation of the first commandment: "You shall have no other gods before me." The issue is not that Israel has rejected God and embraced an idol; the issue, rather, is that Israel wants to have its relationship with God and to serve an idol too. Yet that is the very essence of sin: for God is a jealous God and will under no conditions accept any accommodation. Elijah immediately proposes a contest that will force a decision: yes or no. He tells Ahab to summon the whole people of Israel to Mount Carmel and to bring with him all the priests of Baal and Asherah, a Canaanite goddess of fortune and happiness sponsored by Queen Jezebel. When they arrive, Elijah castigates the gathered community. "How long will you limp along between two views, like a person on unequal legs? Either God is Lord, or Baal; you must decide." Total silence pervades the crowd.

It is easy to catalogue the crises that face the universal church in our time. Financial difficulties are widespread throughout all denominations; ecclesiastical bureaucracies are choked with uncertainty and aimlessness; theological education is drifting aimlessly in whatever direction the fads of culture wish to take it. But there are also times to ask: Why is it in such horrible shape? The answer is suggested by our text for today. The service of Christ will never permit shared time with human ideology, whether it be liberal or conservative. The church may fool itself; it may successfully convince itself that its political and cultural agenda are mandated from heaven and blessed from above. But God will not be fooled. He does not want help in carrying out his objectives; he wants eager obedience in conformity to his revealed will. Human ideology and obedience to God are mutually exclusive, and the church in the end must decide.

Elijah presses the issue even further. He describes a contest that will make the choice clear. His description gives every possible advantage to his opponent, as if to make sure that the outcome can be in no doubt. He states that he stands alone in the execution of his sacred office, while a huge majority minister to Baal. He invites the priests of Baal to choose two steers for sacrifice and to select one of the two for themselves. Each in turn, the prophets of Baal and Elijah will prepare their sacrifices and invoke their God to send fire to ignite it. Whichever God responds with flame is the true God of Israel. Everyone quickly agrees that it is a fair contest. The prophets of Baal go first. They cut up the steer, place it on the wood of the altar, and begin their summons of Baal. The vigil lasts all morning and is accompanied by ceremonial dance; but not a whisper is heard from above. Elijah taunts the failure of their misplaced confidence: "Maybe this Baal of yours is off tending to other business, or maybe he is temporarily unavailable. Who knows, maybe he's taking a nap, and needs a wake-up call?" They carry their fervor to extremes, cutting themselves in the pagan manner with knives and spears until the blood flows freely. But there is nothing but cold, deafening silence.

Why are human ideologies so totally bankrupt? Why are they so completely unable to deliver what they promise? Communism promises a classless society in a people's paradise; yet it has given the world nothing but brutal tyranny and egregious human ruin. Capitalism promises a world of complete self-fulfillment; yet it has ruthlessly stolen away the very heart of human life, which is joy. The reason for the utter failure of all human ideology is that it seeks to solve the problems human beings face, without solving the ultimate problem, which is

humankind itself. There is only one answer to the riddle all human beings pose for themselves. The service of Christ alone is perfect fulfillment, perfect peace, perfect beauty, perfect joy. Christ's commandments are a steadier guide to daily life than all the books ever written
and all the thoughts ever formulated. The law of Christ is better than
life itself and blankets the entire universe with eternal glory.

Now it is Elijah's turn. He does not take the easy way out; if anything, he goes out of his way to make success more difficult. First, he
has the people come closer, so that they can see exactly what he is doing. The traditional altar for Israel's worship has been demolished, so
he carefully rebuilds it one stone at a time. He uses twelve stones in all
to represent the twelve tribes of Jacob, after whom the people Israel is
named. He digs a deep ditch around the reconstructed altar, prepares
the steer, and places it upon the wood. He commands that four water
jars be filled with water and emptied upon the altar; then again; and
then again. Everything is completely soaked: the animal carcass, the
wood, the altar itself. Then he fills the ditch itself with water. When
the time for the regular evening sacrifice arrives, Elijah offers a prayer.
It contains no hysterics; instead, it is a calm and confident appeal to
the God of the fathers of Israel to make known his claim upon his people and to certify the calling of Elijah himself. Immediately, fire from
heaven incinerates the sacrifice, the wood, the altar, even the dust, and
causes all the water in the trench instantly to evaporate. A decision is
forced, and the people respond: "The Lord is God, the Lord is God." Elijah tells them to arrest the false prophets, and they are put to death.
Not one is allowed to slip away.

The blessing of God upon his people is not an occasional token of
favor when life takes a bad turn. Every atom of our existence comes to
us directly from God's gracious hand. He gives us children, and that in
itself is more happiness than can be calculated; but he also gives us
time to enjoy their laughter, their pleasures, their growth, their triumphs. These are unspeakable gifts, any one of which is worth a thousand worlds. He not only gives us a career and a paycheck; he gives us
challenges to the mind, with the fantastic thrill of giving our best effort
to meet each day's assignments. He not only gives us a body to move
around in; he has made us physical creatures, with a splendid creation
to explore, and with goals of exercise and fitness to achieve. No human

ideology has ever given us a single thing; these all come from God, and from God alone. We owe them nothing; we owe him everything.

A point has been made that even King Ahab can't ignore completely. Elijah tells Ahab to fortify himself, for the rains are about to come roaring in. While Ahab eats and drinks, Elijah ascends to the top of Mount Carmel and bows down to pray for rain. He sends his servant to look toward the sea for a rain cloud, but he sees nothing. He sends him back seven times, until finally he reports sighting a small thunderhead in the distance. Then Elijah sends his servant to tell Ahab to harness his chariot and leave, if he doesn't want to get stranded on the mountain. Even as they speak, the skies darken, the winds are whipped up, and a furious storm is unleashed. After three years, rain returns to Israel. Ahab heads for the city of Jezreel; but Elijah, strengthened by God, runs before Ahab and beats him to his destination.

Brothers and sisters, it is God himself who wins the battles of faith that we all must face. His victories are not narrow escapes from desperate situations. They are resounding and comprehensive defeats of all that contradict his gracious purpose in human life. He not only supplies what is lacking for our welfare; he brings into our lives gift after gift, all of which broaden our grasp of the scope of his majesty. He not only protects us from dangers that imperil our well-being; he actively intervenes on our behalf to hold evil at bay, so that every detail of our existence yields maximum benefit. Let us seek not only to appreciate every one of the many blessings in life we've been given. Let us give our highest effort to turn every resource that we can find into active service of God. He deserves nothing less than the very best we have to offer.

3. 1 Kings 19

We continue today our series of sermons based on the prophet Elijah. We began our series by looking at the call of Elijah to preach divine judgment to Israel because of Israel's idolatry. Israel had been led into the false worship of Baal by King Ahab, and it was Elijah's task to call all Israel to account. He announced a nationwide drought, but he was personally protected by God when the rains stopped. Then he prompted a confrontation with the prophets of Baal, and Israel was forced to decide whom it would worship. After fire fell from heaven upon Elijah's sacrifice, he prayed for the rains to return and they did. We considered the contemporary challenge to the church to embrace with single-minded devotion the message of the gospel, to the exclusion of all human ideology. Now, despite his triumph over the prophets of Baal, Elijah's troubles are not over. Ahab is still on the loose; and behind Ahab stands the scheming, evil Queen Jezebel. Elijah's problems have only just begun. Brothers and sister, hear the Word of God.

The fundamental weakness of Ahab is quickly highlighted by the text. Despite the fact that he is king over Israel, he functions as a mere messenger boy for Queen Jezebel. Ahab is responsible for his own acts of treachery, but it is clearly Jezebel who runs the show. Ahab tells Jezebel about the contest between Elijah and the prophets of Baal on Mount Carmel, and how Elijah put to death every one of the prophets. She wastes no time in formulating a response; she pledges herself to the absolute destruction of Elijah. She sends a messenger to Elijah to announce her murderous intent. When he realizes the extent of her rage, he runs for his life. He heads south, out of the northern kingdom of Israel, which is ruled by Ahab, and into the southern kingdom of Judah, beyond Ahab's jurisdiction. He leaves his servant in the southern city of Beersheba, but Elijah himself continues on alone, straight into the wilderness.

The crime of Jezebel quickly unfolds in the form of a plot on Elijah's life. But as is often the case in the Old Testament, her evil deed is part of a complex chain of sinful acts, acts that grow increasingly violent. She is the chief supporter of idolatry in Israel. When Elijah forces the issue of obedience, she takes it personally and uses her influence to carry out a private vendetta. The witness of Scripture, and particularly the Old Testament, uncovers the darkest corners of the human heart. Sin is not an isolated act of wrong-doing; it involves a complicated set of psychological, sociological, and historical factors. The power of human desire is all-consuming in its scope. The answer to temptation in any form is to walk away and never once look back.

Elijah does not stop at the edge of the wilderness but flees deep into the heart of the desert. All he can find for shade is a solitary broom shrub. He collapses in exhaustion and lets loose a bitter cry of frustration. He tells God that he has had enough. He wants it all to end right here and now. He complains that his entire ministry has been a failure; he desires death rather than a single day more of such misery. He falls asleep and receives the divine answer to his prayer. An angel gently nudges him awake and tells him to have something to eat. Elijah glances around, and he discovers within arm's reach a cake of bread baked on a fire and a jug of water. He finishes off both bread and water and returns to sleep. Again the angel wakes him and tells him to take some more nourishment, for he has a long journey ahead of him without food or water. Elijah obeys the angel and then sets out for the long trip across the desert to Mount Sinai in the far south.

We all face the struggle of faith, and we will continue to do so throughout this life. Which of us has not gone through moments of sheer despair: when fear of circumstances beyond our control reaches a fever pitch; when our mental and physical resources are completely done in; when our hope for tomorrow has all but disappeared? These are not easy times, but the path of discipleship shows us how to deal with them. Care of the body is an essential component of the Christian life. If difficulties threaten to become overwhelming, your first reaction should be to make sure that you are doing all you can do to maintain your physical well-being. Why? Why do we as Christians place such a high priority upon the human body? Because we believe that God's Spirit dwells within us and that his presence fills our entire existence in every dimension. We are fortunate to live at a time when medical science has given us a clear description of proper care of the human body. The Christian gospel is a challenge to turn that knowledge into daily practice.

Elijah continues his flight from Jezebel as far away as he can possibly get, and he arrives at Mount Sinai in the southern tip of the Sinai Peninsula. This is holy ground, for it is the very mountain upon which Moses received the Ten Commandments. Elijah finds a place to camp in a nearby cave, where he is addressed directly by God himself. God asks him why he has come to Mount Sinai. Elijah tells him the whole story: he has done everything in his power to honor God's name; but the people of Israel have abandoned their oath of loyalty to God, have desecrated the proper worship of God, and have put to death every prophet who protests. He is the last one alive who sees what is going on, and now they are out to destroy him, too. God responds to Elijah's recital of events by telling him to come out of his cave and ascend the holy mountain in God's very presence. God causes a shattering wind, which tears the mountain apart and breaks the cliffs in pieces, but Elijah cannot find God's presence in the wind; the same process is repeated with an earthquake and with fire, but God cannot be found there either. The lovely irony of God's response is clear only when we remember that he once appeared to Moses in the thunder and the fire on this very mountain. Elijah has clearly expected to see a similar performance; but God will not oblige. Instead, Elijah hears a low whisper, and that whisper contains the living reality of God. God will not be boxed in, and he clearly enjoys a good surprise.

There is no reason whatsoever to deny the action of God in the past. Many in this congregation have lived through times of incredible historical upheaval, when the call of discipleship has demanded direct participation in world-changing events. Faithful Christians have answered that call to duty. But no one era of the church's life can be used to establish a pattern of measurement for every other era. Many today are looking to the great events of world history to find the presence of God. But they are looking in the wrong place. The cutting edge for the future of the church is the realm of everyday life in the world. The true reality of Christian discipleship is forged in daily practice. What have often been treated in the past as mundane matters by the Christian witness — our use of talents and opportunities, our relationship to our family, our effort to carry out the tasks we've been given to do — are now more clearly seen to be at the very heart of the divine will for human good. What was once overlooked is now center-stage in the light of God's eternal presence.

Elijah hears the barely audible whisper of God. He wraps his cloak around his head and emerges from the cave to stand at the entrance. Once again, God asks why he is here, using exactly the same words as before. Once again Elijah answers, repeating the tale of woe he has already told. Despite the lesson that has been learned, the historical situation has not changed, and Elijah needs to know where to go from here. God gives him the commission that is now his to accomplish. From now on, Elijah's concern is to be with the leadership of the future. He is to retrace his steps to the north, where he is to anoint Hazael king over

Syria, Jehu king over Israel, and Elisha as his own replacement. All three will be relentless opponents of God's enemies. However, despite his concern for the future, Elijah is reminded by God that the present is not without its own sources of blessing. Plenty of people in Israel have refused to worship Baal, remaining true to the faith of their fathers.

Brothers and sisters, we live by hope. And it is crucial to that hope to remember the mysterious paradox of the church's historical existence. When it has lived through the best of times, it has experienced the most disappointing results. But when it has gone through the worst of times, it has received the most astonishing gifts. A new generation of the church is growing up before our very eyes. The gift of a future is worth infinitely more than any pains we have suffered in the past. In the meantime, let us not forget that we are not the only ones to suffer. The sad failure of the church in our time has bothered a lot of ordinary people, many of whom will simply not go along with the gimmicks and slogans that come from left and right. Instead, let us remember the unpredictable verve of God's way in human life. Only the foolish count him out in desperate times. The wise always recall that God does not only the impossible but also the utterly unexpected, for the sake of his love.

4. 1 Kings 21

We continue today our series of sermons based on the figure of Elijah. Last week we observed a major lesson that Elijah himself learned in the course of his ministry. While the work of God in the past is fully real and remains completely in effect, nevertheless the way of God in the present cannot be determined based on comparison with the past. While it is the same God who acts, his deeds in human life are full of unanticipated glory. The path of obedience is to follow the divine leading into the future. We considered the fresh attention to daily life that our own age of the church has ushered in. In our reading for today, the treachery of Ahab and Jezebel reaches its deepest extent. And Elijah castigates their evil deed with unbounded fury. Brothers and sisters, hear the Word of God.

There is a vineyard very close to the palace of King Ahab in Jezreel.

It is owned by a citizen of the city named Naboth. But the king desires to own it, so he abruptly and rudely informs Naboth that he must either trade it for another plot of land or sell it for the going price. No basis is given for Ahab's claim upon the vineyard, other than the simple fact that he wants it because it is close by. Naboth adamantly refuses to bargain, and he gives a clear and simple reason. The vineyard has been passed down in his family for generations. No money, nor any substitute, could be worth the treasure of a family legacy. King Ahab returns to his palace sullen and resentful. He is enraged at the unwillingness of Naboth to let go of something that he wants. He throws a royal tantrum, retiring to his bed and refusing to eat or see visitors in childish protest.

How does the sin of Ahab and Jezebel begin? What are its origins? The text of Scripture paints a very clear picture of a man who wants what he does not have, simply because it belongs to someone else. Doubtless Ahab, as the king of Israel, has access to more land and more goods than he could ever possibly use. But he does not have Naboth's land, and that is enough to crush his enjoyment of life. The desire to have, simply because others have, is an unspeakable menace to the rich pleasure of human existence. On the one hand, if acted upon, it leads down a road to certain self-destruction. On the other hand, it blinds us to the incredible reality of what we do have. When such a desire strikes us, we should bury it as soon as it appears. We should redouble our effort to derive the greatest possible delight from the astonishing gifts that we've been given.

Ahab is pouting in his room, and Jezebel comes to find out what is wrong. She asks him why he is so upset, and he tells her about his confrontation with Naboth. Jezebel reminds him of his royal office, with the clear implication that nothing is to be withheld from the king. He should bounce back up and return to good cheer, for she will take care of everything. The text describes her subsequent actions in detail. She instigates a very clever ploy to destroy Naboth, and thus to gain his land for her husband. She writes to the leading citizens and tells them to make Naboth the chief of the city in a special ceremony. But right at that point, when Naboth is in the public limelight, two paid informants are to come forward and to accuse him of the capital crime of blasphemy and sedition. Then he is to be executed. The leaders of the city carry out the script exactly as Jezebel has written it. Overnight, the character of innocent Naboth is horribly defamed, and his very life is taken away. Jezebel returns to King Ahab to tell him the news of Naboth's death. In a gesture of scarcely concealed gloating, she reports that the man who defied the king is now out of the way; the vineyard is his to enjoy. Ahab gets what he wanted all along.

Clearly, the relationship between Ahab and Jezebel is badly twisted and distorted. It is impossible to determine who is using whom, but both bring out the worst features in the other. Yet the focus of Scripture is in another direction, on the crime of false witness. This story is the supreme instance in the whole Old Testament of the violation of the ninth commandment: "You shall not bear false witness against your neighbor." And it brings out the devastating consequences of such a sin: a helpless man loses his life because of the lies of bribed testimony. The interest of the Bible is not in truth telling as an abstract moral principle; rather, the concern has to do with any form of lying that will harm or destroy a neighbor. Such behavior is not an option for Christians. What does this mean? Luther gave a precise formulation, which still applies even today: "Every report that cannot be adequately proved is false witness." An accusation, however heinous the crime, is not a verdict and should never be treated like one. It is our duty, as Christians, to protect the good name of others. A good reputation is one dimension of the well-being of the whole person in human society, and we are to guard that reputation with as much care as we extend to physical and moral support of others.

When Elijah finds out what has happened, he is livid. He is commanded by God to go and find Ahab in Naboth's vineyard and to deliver a message of divine outrage and overwhelming judgment. He is to tell Ahab that his act of murder and theft has not gone unnoticed, and that Ahab himself will suffer the fate that he has unjustly caused to fall upon Naboth. Elijah approaches Ahab, and Ahab as usual gives a caustic greeting: "I suppose you've been looking for me, old enemy." Elijah agrees that he has been looking for him, for the simple reason that Ahab has completely devoted himself to wrongdoing in the eyes of God. He tells him that God will do nothing but harm to him and his family, that God will utterly obliterate any future legacy that he hopes to leave behind. Every male in Ahab's household will be annihilated.

Jezebel will be food for dogs, and Ahab's entire heritage will be squashed. The roles will be reversed; while Ahab stole from innocent Naboth the inheritance of his family, God himself will wrest away from Ahab all hope for a future.

The severe reaction of Elijah simply underlines the seriousness of the sin of false witness in the testimony of Scripture. And it gives us pause to reflect upon our own good fortune to live in the times in which we live. Despite the fact that no form of human justice is perfect and de-spite the fact that abuse of any legal system is always a possibility, still, the fact is that we live under the extraordinary blessing of a judicial sys-tem bound to the rule of law. No human being, whether rich or poor, whether high or low, is outside the authority of the law. And facts are to be determined by an impartial jury of peers, not by the clever manipula-tion of public opinion. It has not always been so. And even in our own time, equal protection under the law is not a universally acknowledged principle in the societies of the world. But such failures should only deepen our own sense of profound gratitude for the system we have and for the wisdom of those who brought it into being.

The story is being driven to a fatal and ineluctable demise for Ahab and his family. That impression is reinforced by the conclusion, which begins by summarizing everything corrupt about Ahab's life. He stands out, in an already sorry company of wicked kings who perverted the law of God. He weakly acquiesces to his wife's evil tactics. His idolatry is so foul that he is completely indistinguishable from the heathen oc-cupants of Canaan whom God had displaced for Israel's sake. And then, suddenly, the unthinkable happens. When Ahab hears what Eli-jah has to say, he regrets what he has done and shows deep remorse for his sinful deeds. In an astonishing turn of events, Ahab repents. God himself points out to Elijah Ahab's change of heart; it is not a charade, but genuine. God tells Elijah that because of Ahab's contrition, he will delay the execution of his wrath until the next generation.

Brothers and sisters, it is easy to get caught up in analysis of events in the world in which we live. Even as Christians, we remain active participants in the ongoing stream of human life in all its forms. But now and then, it is wise to find our bearings again by the bright star of the gospel. We believe in the forgiveness of sins. Despite the absolute requirement to obey the commands of Christ, at all costs, the gospel of forgiveness frees us from an endless self-torture over mistakes that we have made. We have all made them, and we should leave them in the past where they belong. And the gospel of forgiveness is likewise a steady guide to our relationships with others. No doors should ever be finally closed by us. No doubt we have all been surprised to see changes that we never expected and to witness miraculous transformation of human life under the gracious hand of God. The gospel is a reminder of just how open-ended the future is, and how utterly certain are the grounds for all human hope.

5. 2 Kings 2:1-18

We conclude today our series of sermons based on the prophet Elijah. We have witnessed an incredible life in a difficult time. Time and again, Elijah's courage and audacity have triumphed against overwhelming odds. The story of his ministry has yielded rich insights into the nature of Christian discipleship. But now we come to the final chapter: the death of Elijah. The biblical account of Elijah's death is a passage of exquisite beauty, possessing extraordinary power. It not only describes the final days of an amazing life; it gives brilliant illumination into the very meaning of death itself. Let us consider today the passing from this earth of Elijah the prophet. Brothers and sisters, hear the Word of God.

The description of Elijah's death has two main characters, rather than one: Elijah himself, and Elisha, his successor. Elisha has already been introduced in the narrative a few chapters before our reading, and a summary of his initial appearance is helpful in understanding our text for today. Elijah first encounters Elisha out in the fields plowing. He casts his cloak upon him, thus indicating that he has been chosen as Elijah's replacement. Elisha leaves the field, but he asks Elijah if he can return to kiss his mother and father good-bye. Elijah's response is brusque at best; he tells Elisha to go back home, for they have nothing to do with each other. Instead of returning home, Elisha slaughters his animals and gives them to his neighbors for a feast, and leaves everything to follow Elijah. From the very beginning, the clear issue for Elisha is one of priorities and the absolute demand for obedience.

That theme runs right through the story of Elijah's death, only this time it is Elijah himself who provides the source of temptation for Elisha. They start out from Gilgal to the Jordan, in a kind of funeral procession. But before they even set out, Elijah tells Elisha to wait in Gilgal, while he goes alone to Bethel. Elisha refuses to wait, instead solemnly declaring that he will stay by Elijah's side no matter what. So together they travel to Bethel. Another temptation to Elisha appears in the form of the company of prophets who reside in Bethel. They ask Elisha if he knows what he is getting into, for surely he is aware that Elijah is going to his death. Elisha tells them that of course he knows, but it is not their concern to worry about. Once again, Elijah tells Elisha that he must go alone to Jericho; but once again Elisha refuses to remain behind. And once again, Elisha encounters the group of prophets but rejects their advice. A final time, Elijah declares to Elisha that he must go ahead alone to the river Jordan; Elisha remains unwilling to stay behind. This time, the band of prophets halts some distance from the river and watches the two travel on alone to the river's edge. Elijah takes off his cloak, folds it, strikes the water, and the rivers part in two; Elijah and Elisha cross over on dry ground. Despite the difference in the ministry of Elijah and Moses, the same God parts the waters for both.

The call to discipleship seizes our existence from above and includes within its realm our whole being. Christian faith does not fit neatly into a package of human spirituality. On the contrary, the practice of the Christian life involves all that we are and all that we have: our time, our possessions, our talents, our opportunities, our relationships. The command of Christ cuts straight across every human tie and binds us in direct accountability to the living Lord himself. For every one of us there are temptations to distraction from obeying the commands of Christ. Surely the severest temptations come from those we love and respect the most. Nevertheless, no matter how well-meaning the advice we receive, no matter how noble the source from which it comes, no advice, nor any claim to our attention, outranks the commandment of Christ. Our loyalty to him is lifelong and absolute. Every known blessing in the entire universe lies down one road, and one road only: faithful obedience to Christ's revealed will.

After Elijah and Elisha cross over the Jordan, Elijah himself confirms that Elisha did the right thing in staying with him to the end. He asks Elisha what he can give him, before he goes to meet his death. Elisha is quick to respond: he wants an abundant share of the same prophetic spirit that Elijah himself enjoyed. Elijah tells him that his request is not easily granted; however, it will be given, on condition that Elisha is there at the very last moment of Elijah's earthly journey. Otherwise, Elisha's desire for a measure of Elijah's spirit will be foiled. They continue their conversation, walking along the far bank of the Jordan River together. Suddenly, a flaming chariot pulled by a fiery team of horses passes between them, thrusting them apart. And a whirlwind gathers Elijah up into eternity.

God does not will for your lives isolated moments of temporary victory. Instead, he surrounds your entire existence with eternal blessing. He turns small deeds into enormous contributions to his kingdom. He transforms human effort into a miracle of lasting accomplishment. He plants where nothing has ever grown before, and he brings into being a rich yield that cascades over into the lives of others. He takes away what is harmful to your well-being in life, and he puts in its place the very things you were missing for the greatest possible happiness and pleasure life affords. Small dreams are transfigured by his mercy into magnificent realities. He gives all this and more, and he has already provided many times over for your distant future. But he demands a response, if these blessings are to be received. The call to discipleship is for a lifetime. It doesn't ebb and flow with a changing schedule; it doesn't come and go with differing circumstances. The call of Christ always appears in the eternal Now of his presence.

Elisha is ecstatic with joy at the wonderful sight he has beheld. He calls out to the departing Elijah with deepest affection: "My father, my father." He exclaims the true significance of what has occurred: Elijah has been removed into heaven by the royal procession of God's people. Once Elijah is gone, Elisha never sees a trace of him again. He tears apart his garments, in the universal gesture of grief in ancient times. He picks up Elijah's cloak, which had fallen from him, and returns to the bank of the Jordan River. He repeats the gesture that Elijah himself had only just done: he touches the waters of the river with the cloak. He himself is clearly in some suspense. Will it part? Will God do for him what he once did for Elijah? He quickly receives the answer, as the waters once again move aside to allow him to pass unharmed. The company of prophets sees him return alone across the Jordan River, and they affirm that Elisha has indeed inherited the prophetic spirit of Elijah. They bow to the earth, in an expression of complete reverence.

There is, throughout the Bible, more than one perspective on the reality of death. Clearly one strain of witnesses speaks of death as a divine curse for human sin and a threatening menace to human fulfillment. There are times in the Christian church when the voice of these witnesses must be heard, no matter how challenging this perspective is to our modern sensibilities. But here in the death of Elijah, we hear a very different voice, with a lyrical tone of sheer amazement. Death is not a bitter end to human existence. Instead, we must speak of the sublime dignity of death. A life of distinguished human achievement comes to its conclusion; an earthly pilgrimage is ushered into its eternal home; a waiting servant is translated into the divine embrace. The struggle of faith is swallowed up in total victory. All death brings grief; but in the light of Easter, we cannot conceal the honor and celebration of life that death entails. Death is not the end; it is the triumphant finale of eternal joy.

The story ends on a humorous note, as if to put the crowning touch upon its wondrous contents. The company of prophets, who have seen these events from a distance, want to go in search of Elijah's body. They ask Elisha for permission, but he refuses; they keep badgering him, so he finally gives in, though he refuses to go along himself. They conduct a thorough search, but find nothing. When they return to Elisha, he chides them for ever having gone in the first place.

Brothers and sisters, the glorious reality of Easter faith changes the ridiculous folly of these prophets into a fantastic lesson in truth. Time and again, the Christian church is tempted to misunderstand the witness of Scripture to the resurrection. Eternal life is misconstrued as a form of living memory in others, or as a natural event in the cycle of life, or as the escape of an immortal spirit from a mortal body. None of these ideas has anything to do with the Christian faith. We believe in the resurrection of the body. We believe that God raises the whole person from death, body and soul, and transforms us into the eternal glory of Christ. In the end, the old spiritual had it right: "Swing low, sweet chariot, comin' for to carry me home. . . ."

X

PSALM 4

There is a certain serenity to faith that defies all forms of human calculation; and yet it is more real and lasting than the measurable commodities of this world. Our psalm for today is a perfect description of the peace of mind that comes with trust in the living God. The title of the psalm is this: "to the musical director, a psalm of David." The title reminds us of two facts. First, the prayers of the Psalter are not a pious retreat from reality. No life could be more filled with turmoil and agitation than was that of David. And yet, because they are ascribed to him, the Psalms open up for the reader possibilities for human welfare that are available to every human being, no matter what circumstances life brings along. And second, the prayers of the Psalter are not simply notable expressions of devotion from the ancient past. They are incorporated into a book of prayer, which is itself included within the Scriptures of the church. Ultimately, the voice we hear in the Psalter is the voice of God himself, who uses these prayers to teach us the right way to find what we seek in life. Brothers and sisters, hear the Word of God.

The psalm begins with a simple declaration of desire to be heard in prayer by the almighty God. Even as he addresses God, the Psalmist moves with the ease of intimacy toward the substance of his concern. He approaches God as one who stands in right relation to him; yet he concedes that that relation is established by the initiative of God himself. He takes a moment to remember the changes in his life under the tenderness of divine care. There was a time when his options in life were reduced to zero; yet through the action of God, his life was suddenly filled with infinite possibility. So he asks God once again to be gracious in redemptive love and to provide an answer to the requests he brings. The Psalmist quickly turns to take stock of his situation, even addressing his enemies indirectly, as though they were present to hear. They have made what should have been the good reputation of his character into a source of reproach. They have turned rightful honor into contempt. He asks them how long the disgrace will continue. How long will they pursue an empty scheme? How long will they embrace deception and falsehood?

The voice of the Psalmist then turns to the comfort and instruction of the faithful who join in his prayer. They must recognize that God has not at all abandoned the cause of the Psalmist. Just the opposite, God has set apart those who obey his will for special treatment in life. He has taken them under his own protective wing. For this reason, the Psalmist is confident that whatever he asks from God will be granted to him. This astonishing truth, which applies to all the obedient, is grounds for overwhelming amazement. The enemies of the Psalmist are exhorted to be in awe of the majesty of God and stop sinning. Instead of blaming and criticizing others unfairly, they are to reflect upon events in solitude and remain quiet. They are to carry out the prescribed duties of the life of obedience and to leave in God's hands the management of all concerns in human existence.

The Psalmist closes his prayer with a final declaration of total confidence in God and genuine relaxation of mind and body. He points out that there are plenty of people around who assert that nobody is available to help out the faithful when they are in a corner. Surely, they say, the faithful are isolated, helpless, beyond relief even if there were any who would come to the rescue. But the Psalmist is not perturbed, because he does not look to other people for deliverance. He looks to God alone and asks him to bring near the joy and benevolence of his wondrous presence. That presence changes everything. The Psalmist expresses to God directly what that presence has meant for the overall good of his life. God's presence has brought more sheer happiness into his experience of living than any amount of worldly success could afford. Above all, it has brought relief from every pressure to the human mind. At night, he lies down and falls asleep at once; he does not suffer the tossing and turning of laborious worry. The explanation is simple: God is the sole reason why he dwells securely. No other factors are relevant; for God alone is the source of life-giving peace.

The first point in our reflection upon the psalm this morning must be a brief moment of recognition of the faithfulness of divine care throughout our lives. The psalm speaks of moving from the narrow straits of human distress to a large territory with room to roam and enjoy the range of human experiences. Such a transformation of our circumstances in life does not come about by clever human forethought. None of us here would be willing to claim that our lives have unfolded exactly as we planned them from the beginning. Nor does such a transformation come about by the benign operation of chance in the universe. We have not moved along a quantitative scale from less good to more good; instead, we have moved along a qualitative scale, leaving behind a situation that promises no good whatsoever, finding before us a new world of sheer abundance in every respect. Neither human cleverness nor blind fate accounts for our happiness in life. God alone is the architect of change in human existence. He alone builds our future, according to the exact specifications of his eternal purpose of love. He makes the whole creation a home in which we grow, create, dream, and accomplish. God alone is the maker of human happiness.

Our second point must be an attempt to capture in our imagination how truly marvelous beyond words is the divinely given opportunity of prayer. We all face threats to our well-being, whether in the form of radical evil in the world, resistance to the divine purpose in the universal church, or our own frailty in life. How will we cope with the myriad dangers that would undo us? While there are many dangers, there is only one right response to every single one of them: to ask God to remove all obstacles from the path that lies ahead of us. And he will do it. Scarcely can we believe so great a promise, and yet God has shown throughout the entire course of our lives that it is a promise he will keep in every conceivable contingency. He hears when we ask for help; he alters the reality of the universe to bring us whatever aid we require; he acts even beyond our expectation to bring about perfect fulfillment in every dimension of our lives. So great is his love toward us — undeserved, yet filled with the splendor of absolute sovereignty over all things.

Our third point is to acknowledge what it is that we are given to do. We are not to manage the affairs of the universe, which is just as well, because we could not possibly carry out that role. Nor are we to assume responsibility for the actions of others. Again, if we try to act for others, our good intentions will only make matters worse in the end. But what we not only can do but must do is to carry out those obligations in life that God has laid upon us. Our family requires, not a little time and effort now and then, but a constant outpouring of affection and affirmation in all aspects of living. Our work demands, not a dutiful display of exertion, but the best energies of devoted passion that we can pour into it. Our friendships are in need of, not an occasional suitable confirmation, but an undying loyalty that transcends whatever resistance may come along. The world in which we live deserves, not a grudging awareness of time passing, but a serious and thoughtful engagement with human culture in a desperate and needy time. These we can manage, because God himself has given us to do them. But as for the rest, God alone must bring it to pass.

Our final point is a due consideration of the majestic proportion of the divine gifts. It is certainly true to say that money cannot buy the qualities of human joy that pervade our everyday experience of living. Yet that is not the half of it. The wealth of the whole universe does not begin to compare with the unrestrained giggle of a child. The combined achievements of all human endeavor do not in the least measure up to the thrill of a good challenge, straining every fiber of our being to meet it. No amount of human renown and public acclaim even comes close to the warm affection of a familiar friend, the kind voices of cherished companions in life. Admire as we do the distinguished monuments of human progress in the past, what times can compare with the excitement of the present? God has created us to flourish upon the earth that he made good for human benefit. He made us for life; and he renews the earth, day by day, to sustain us in untroubled contentment.

Brothers and sisters, we not only live in the best of all possible worlds; we advance from one perfection to another through the generosity of divine compassion. Let our hearts be full, our minds at rest, our bodies tranquil, and our wills determined to embrace the knowledge of God. He is the true spring of all satisfaction.

XI

FROM 1 CORINTHIANS

1. 1 Corinthians 1

We begin today a series of sermons based upon Paul's first letter to the Corinthians. This letter is written from the perspective of the power of the risen Christ over all the nations of the world. Jesus Christ, crucified and risen, is the one hope of all the earth. The church belongs to him in body and mind, and the authority of the apostle Paul for faith and practice is grounded directly in the sovereign rule of Christ. Indeed, the opening verses make clear that the authority of Paul extends unchanged to every age of the church, and therefore to our very own. The problems that Paul brings to the attention of the church at Corinth all revolve around a single paradox. On the one hand, the church already lives in the new age of redemption in joyful service to Christ. Sin is in the past; newness of life in the Spirit has blossomed. Yet, on the other hand, Christians live out the claim of discipleship in the old world of human rebellion. They cannot escape the horizon of the world. The tension that this paradox creates for Christian existence can never be erased in this life, and sustained effort is needed to observe its subtlety. Brothers and sisters, hear the Word of God.

The letter begins with a rich word of greeting and thanksgiving. The apostleship of Paul is received from Christ according to God's sovereign purpose. The letter comes, not as interesting chit-chat, but as the command of Christ to the Christians of Corinth — and to all Chris-

127

tians everywhere. Every word that follows is based on the good news of God's redeeming love in Christ. Paul professes his affection for the local church at Corinth and acknowledges the present reality of God's gracious care in their midst. Their lives have been transformed through witness to Christ. They are not missing any of the divine gifts that upbuild the church in wondrous blessing. The eye of faith among the Corinthian Christians is fixed upon the final return of Christ, and Paul expresses his confidence that their lives will always reflect the requirements of discipleship. They cannot fail, for their life together is called into being by the electing love of God, through personal encounter with the risen Lord, Jesus Christ.

A small church has a capacity to reveal what a large church can often conceal. How does God bring a congregation to a mature faith? How does he expand its witness to the community that surrounds it? How does he give it growth over time? Such growth comes not through clever programs or expensive gimmicks but rather through the extraordinary gifts of his Spirit in the lives of ordinary people. The gift of music turns the choir into a chorus of angels. The dedication of Sunday school teachers gives birth to a new generation of the faith. The creativity of church workers turns routine events into causes for celebration. Simple acts of kindness and mercy bring moral support to the weary. The everyday lives of Christian disciples yield incalculable influence for good in human life. Witness to Christ is born in word and deed; seeds are planted; and now and then, a new plant sprouts with fresh gifts to share.

Paul is not insincere in his opening word of encouragement; but he does not wait long to express his deep concern. This is not simply a personal matter for Paul, but an exercise of his apostolic office. He admonishes the Corinthians to exhibit at all times a unity of purpose and conviction. He spells out in detail what he means. He has received reliable information that various parties have formed schisms in the church. There is a Paul party, and a Cephas party, and an Apollos party, and a Christ party. Yet such schisms are inadmissible where Christ is worshiped. There is one Christ, therefore there is one church; the very notion of a party within the church is abhorrent. Paul makes it clear that he has done nothing to encourage a personal following of his own among the Corinthians. Such a following would directly contradict the sacred calling of his ministry to proclaim Christ to all the earth. Any effort to use his office to gain a personal entourage would invalidate his entire message.

Let us now move back from the microcosm of a small church to the macrocosm of modern Christianity. And here we, too, must move from profound delight to grave concern. The politicization of the gospel in modern Christianity has clearly created a vast schism in the contemporary church. There are those Christians who are sure that God is on the side of the Republicans; there are others who are equally sure that God is on the side of the Democrats. Both are wrong; for both assume to know what no human being can know. But their self-delusion is not benign; it is in fact a malignant force for destruction of all that is good in the Christian community. Efforts to root it out have thus far failed, for everywhere conservative Christians fall into the one trap, while liberal Christians fall into the other. The gospel message is fundamentally altered where these mistakes are made, so that the faith once delivered to the saints and cherished for generations of Christians as their dearest possession is in jeopardy of its very life. To politicize the gospel is to withdraw from the unity of Christ.

Paul expands his point about church division and shows its true basis. The genuine preaching of Christ is scorned by the unbelieving world, but to the redeemed it is the energy for life supplied by God himself. There is nothing new about this; already the Old Testament teaches that God's wisdom confounds all earthly pretensions. Paul mocks all would-be know-it-alls, whether highly trained experts, armchair philosophers, or simple rabble-rousers: none of them has the least inkling of the truth. God never intended the world to find him through its own superior understanding. The wisdom of God is contained in the foolishness of proclamation, which confers slavation on all who embrace it. One half of humanity, the Jews, try to find God through pious moments of inspiration; the other half, the Gentiles, try to find God through clever manipulation of ideas. Neither knows the gospel, which teaches the atoning death of Christ for all humanity, something the Jews are unable to accept and the Gentiles are unwilling even to consider. But to those whom God has summoned, the preaching of Christ is the focus of all truth and all strength. Jews and Gentiles chatter away; God in Christ has changed the world.

Hand in hand with the spread of politics in the church has come

129

the heresy of human values, both conservative and liberal. Conservative values tell us: "Work hard, follow the rules, and you will achieve the good life in the end." Liberal values tell us: "Break down the walls that separate human beings, and a new, classless society of human liberation will emerge." These claims, left and right, are an evil lie. What does the gospel tell us? You cannot put yourself right with God, whether through hard work or through high ideals. There is only one hope for you to embrace: the free gift of new life through the cross of Christ. He died, in your place, so that you might live. You do not need to search your own past for the clue to existence; the starting point of every day you live is the death of Christ for all your sins. You do not need to guarantee your future to prove your worth; each day is a gift to be enjoyed, and the future leads to God's redeeming love. Jesus Christ died for your sins: that is your joy, that is your hope, that is your reason for living, that is your future, that is the first and the last word about your entire life endeavor.

The content of the gospel, Paul tells the Corinthians, is mirrored in the electing grace of God. Look around you, he says, and see: Where are the powerful public officials? Where are the high-born? Where are the learned experts? God has shined the light of Christ upon the base, the low, the insignificant, even upon the despised things of this earth, in order to put to shame the high and the mighty. He has intentionally chosen the weak in order to defeat the strong. Indeed, he has elected things that have no quantifiable existence in order to nullify the existing order of things. Why? What is the purpose for these strange ways of the Almighty? So that no human being can ever have any legitimate grounds to boast before God. Unity with Christ fulfills every human need — for understanding of God's will, for justification, for growth in the Christian faith, and for eternal life. Nothing is left over as a ground for human self-justification.

Brothers and sisters, the politics of values is a systematic pattern of betrayal, deception, and cynical manipulation of public opinion. These ideologies have the appearance of wisdom, because they are supported by all the vast resources of modern culture, whether in communication, social science, or technology. But they are a mask for hypocrisy and depraved immorality. Yet there is a single word, loved by Christians the world over, which is more powerful than all values combined.

And that word is the truth. We do not live by slogans or ideologies; we live by the word of Christ, which is the truth. We do not cave in to public pressure; we obey the truth, which is the command of Christ. We do not allow human integrity to slip through our fingers unnoticed, because we are focused upon the truth: the claim of Christ. Jesus Christ is God's gift of truth to the whole earth. Let all the earth remain silent before him.

2. 1 Corinthians 5

We continue today our series of sermons based upon 1 Corinthians. In the opening chapter, Paul lays the basis for all that follows in the letter. He begins with a blistering attack upon the ideologies of this world, which have caused schism and conflict among the Corinthian Christians. The gospel, by contrast, is the end of all human ideology, teaching to all the world the truth of God's love through the cross of Christ. We considered last week the malignant spread of politics in the church, both conservative and liberal. Whoever pretends to know the divine perspective on the upcoming election is a fool; and whoever listens to a fool is an even greater fool. We also observed the underlying ideology of values, both capitalist and egalitarian, which fuels the heresies of both the left and the right. The preaching of the cross is the end of all human ideologies, which too often serve only as a screen for vile human behavior. In our chapter for today, Paul uses the framework he has laid down to address a particularly troublesome test case in Corinth. Brothers and sisters, hear the Word of God.

The tone of this chapter is clearly one of outrage. Paul is angry enough at the instance of immorality that he mentions; but if anything he is even more angry at the reaction of the Corinthian Christians. What is the situation? Paul has received a report that one of the church members in Corinth has crossed every conceivable line of acceptable conduct. There is no controversy concerning the facts of the case; Paul addresses the problem as a well-known state of affairs that is hidden from no one. It is not simply a question of adultery; rather, the man in question has entered into a sexual relationship with his own stepmother. Not even a depraved pagan would consider such an act; indeed, Roman law forbade such a relationship, as did certainly the Old Testament. The man has stepped outside of the boundaries of ethical integrity from every possible moral standpoint. The fact of the man's immoral activity is in itself supremely unsettling.

But the animus of Paul's reaction is fed from another source: namely, the way the church at Corinth has handled the matter. They are proud of their spiritual community; they have put on airs about their accomplishments and achievements; they have boasted of their attractive circumstances. Paul is aghast. How can they be conceited, when they should be deeply disturbed and disquieted? They have only one course to take: to remove the man from their fellowship. Paul does not need to be there on the spot to make up his mind; the facts of the case speak for themselves, and there is no room whatsoever for ethical maneuvering. Again, Paul is not giving his own personal opinion here, or even his opinion as an apostle; he is delivering the verdict of Christ himself that the man must be directly confronted for his own good. Paul lays it on the line; the conceited attitude of the Corinthians is the source of all their trouble. They have forgotten a basic and obvious truth: that one example of horrific misconduct can spread and affect everything and everyone in the church. He uses the analogy of the Eucharist to symbolize the newness of life that is required of all who lay claim to Christ. The aim of Christian existence is the celebration of life with pure love for the truth, not with depraved wickedness.

No one can deny the confusion that presently afflicts the universal church. Nowhere is this more clearly seen than in the question of human sexuality. Simple truths, basic truths concerning the requirement of lifelong fidelity in marriage are treated as matters of controversy. The most obvious norms of Christian conduct are handled as if they are unclear or vague. How has this state of affairs come about?

The first answer I would suggest is the modern peddling of cheap grace. Cheap grace means that the church too hastily announces the message of forgiveness; any sin can be overlooked, no transformation of human life is demanded, no accountability is required. The church seems to pass out free tickets to whoever asks. The worst culprit here, I must hasten to add, is modern Christian preaching. Modern preaching has all but lost the notion of requirements for Christian living. It expects nothing, and so it gets what it expects. But in so doing, it has lost all contact with the traditional preaching of the church, and indeed with Scripture itself. The grace of the gospel costs us everything we are and have.

The second answer I would give is that much of modern Christianity has ignored the struggle of faith against temptation. Conservative theology wants to build a world where there is no temptation. Conservatives want to return to a puritanical universe where morality is legislated for everyone, and therefore all causes for temptation are removed. But that is clearly not the solution Paul has in mind. He explicitly forbids a perfectionistic attempt to remold society after the Christian image. Liberal theology wants to relax altogether the tension that the Christian necessarily feels in relation to the world. If there are opportunities for sin in the world, then the Christian idea of sin must be reinterpreted to fit them in. If the morals of the world drastically change, then the Christian church must keep up with drastic changes of its own. But again, Paul explicitly forbids just such a relaxation of the moral life. Faith is always a struggle. Every Christian continues to live in the world and is free in Christ to enjoy to the full what can be enjoyed. A puritanical denunciation of common gifts of life is a denial of the gospel. But no Christian is ever free from the obligation owed to the commandments of Christ. Such "freedom" is sheer bondage. If the whole world says yes, and Christ says no, the answer is always no.

The third answer I would give is that many Christians today, left and right, have lost their sense of joy. The commandments of Christ are not a burden to be tolerated; they are the perfect gift of a gracious Lord, whose ultimate purpose is that you soak up from creation every last drop of happiness and pleasure that it contains. He sets limits for your life, not in order to withhold from you something precious, but in order to show you exactly where you can find everything you've always wanted, and even more than you ever knew was there. He sets a direction for your life, not because he wants to dash your hopes, but because he wants every skill he's given you to be shown to the whole world; because he wants you to succeed, in ways that you never knew to dream; because he wants you to win in a race that you never knew to run. He establishes a pace for your life, because he knows the frailty of time; he knows the dangers of moving too fast or too slow, and he knows the infinite rewards of steady movement toward the goals ahead. The commandments of Christ are the joy of the earth; whoever obeys them knows the source of every satisfaction in existence.

The final answer I would give is that much of modern Christianity, left and right, has forgotten Christ. Many Christians today look to Scripture to find support for ideological dogma; but in so doing, they have closed their ears to the voice of Christ, which fills every corner of mind and body with sheer loveliness. They look to values to anchor human existence, and so they cut themselves off from Christ himself, who is the firmest support any human being can receive, a perfect stay through any trial, an unwavering brace through every conflict of life. They look to forms of self-improvement to expand their grasp on the good life; and so they overlook the Lord of life, who became a human being in order to show us step-by-step how to take in the vast panorama of God's good creation. They look to self-justification to affirm their place in this world; and so they never receive the astonishing gift of new life in the service of Christ, which demands everything that we have to give, and offers in return the imperishable dignity of the cross. To forget Christ is to forget how to live; to discover him is to come alive for the first time.

Brothers and sisters, we have focused upon the causes of the troubles afflicting modern Christianity; but we must return briefly in closing to the symptoms. Paul mentions the case of a sexually immoral person, and he closes the chapter with an exhortation to the Corinthian Christians to sever their relationship to him. Surely the modern church has seen enough of the dangers of appeasement in the past; let us not be fooled in the present. If you give in to one who abuses his authority, you may think you buy a little peace of mind, a little period of rest to gather your strength, a little time to settle your affairs. But in fact you gain nothing; you only give that person another chance to perpetrate his crime upon yet another victim. You gain nothing, and you lose everything: your freedom, your honor, and ultimately your very self. The answer of the church to such a person is no! never! under no circumstances! no more! As hard as it is, the simple act of courage is the key to every future blessing.

3. 1 Corinthians 12

We continue today our series of sermons based upon the book of 1 Corinthians. In our chapter for last week, Paul delivered a scathing rebuke
to the Christians in Corinth for their failure to react appropriately to a
situation of notorious misconduct. We examined the problems afflicting modern Christianity, both conservative and liberal, and spoke of
the perils of cheap grace, the relaxation of the struggle of faith, the loss
of joy, and the ignorance of Christ that characterizes the modern
church. In our text for today, Paul focuses his attention upon the positive side of church life in Corinth: the abundance of gifts they have received from God's Spirit. Brothers and sisters, hear the Word of God.

Paul does two things in this chapter: he holds up a mirror to the
church in Corinth so that they can see how truly blessed they are; and
he endeavors to explain to them how to cultivate and apply the many
blessings they have received. He not only wants them to have the gifts
of the Spirit; he also wants them to use those gifts in an effective way.
But first he reminds them that spiritual gifts are part of the comprehensive change in human existence that comes with Christian faith. The
Christians of Corinth have left behind a past that belongs altogether in
the past; a time in which they, too, shared the pagan environment of
the ancient world, irresistibly and repeatedly drawn toward voiceless
idols. It is crucial to understand that spiritual gifts must never be applied to an idolatry that belongs to a former mode of life. The certain
test of whether spiritual gifts have been misapplied centers around the
person of Christ. Speaking against Christ is not to exercise gifts of
God's Spirit; but affirming the sole rule of Christ over the entire universe is rightly to exercise those gifts.

Many new resources have been offered by both conservative and
liberal Christians; but Scripture provides the sure rule of faith by
which to discern whether they are being used for the purpose for
which they are intended. Both the religious left and the religious right
have produced new hymns, new prayers, new modes of preaching,
new translations of the Bible, new forms of church scholarship. But in
many cases, the same patterns are repeated. First, human values are affirmed; the conservatives stress the nostalgia of a golden age in the
past, while the liberals stress the agenda of a new age in the future.

Then every aspect of Christianity is reinterpreted to fit into the liberal or conservative mold; if it doesn't fit it is changed, excised, or simply ignored. What comes out on the other end has a hollow ring of Christian witness; but in truth it has lost the substance. Values do not lead to Christ; they lead, left and right, back to the old age of human rebellion. Values squash human creativity, forcing everyone to conform to the dull standard of a political ideology. Values are idols; any use of human creativity to serve them is effort wasted upon folly.

How do we rightly use the astonishing resources that God's Spirit has planted in the church? That is the question Paul now raises for the Corinthian Christians. The foundation for the answer is a dazzling paradox: no matter how great the variety of talents, they are all the fruits of the one Spirit of God. No matter how wide the range of duties Christians undertake, they are all given by the one Christ. No matter how extensive the activities of Christians, the one God produces them all. The paradox of the community of faith is grounded in the mystery of God: God is a unity within a diversity of functions; so also the plurality of gifts serves the one common good. That means that every individual Christian contributes to the life of the whole by doing best what he or she has been given by God's Spirit to do. Paul steps back for a moment and samples the incredible array of gifts in the community of faith: gifts of proclamation and theological education, care for the needy, church administration, helpful deeds for others, church leadership. All come from the one divine Spirit, who distributes to each according to his gracious purpose for the whole.

I do not need to stress to this congregation what everyone who knows you clearly observes: the beauty of the Spirit that shines on every face and every deed. You are a supremely gifted people. But now I ask: How will you, as an individual in this congregation, make the contribution that you want to make? The first point is that all comparisons between yourself and other people are useless. You cannot find your own voice, your own purpose, your own strengths, by measuring them against the corresponding gifts of others. To seek to be exactly like others is to squelch the very variety that God's Spirit makes possible. Enjoy the variety but focus on the unique, and you will be the blessing for others that you hope to be. Second, do not fear the presence of human personality in the exercise of God's gifts. The last thing the church needs is lifeless conformity to a human image of proper conduct. If you have interests, pursue them with gusto; if you have opportunities, use them with passion; if you have goals, chase them with abandon; if you have new ideas, test them out without fear. You will not detract one bit from the life of the community by being yourself; on the contrary, you will only add to it. And third, do not underestimate the gifts that you've been given. Especially in our troubled times there is a great need for a fresh approach to all dimensions of church life. At no time has human creativity been less apparent in the universal church; at no time has it been more essential.

Paul produces an extended metaphor to broaden the issue he has raised for the Corinthian Christians. He compares the church to a human body. His point is completely missed if one mishears his image as a comparison to a social organization. Rather, his point is that the entire existence of the community is grounded directly in Christ. Just as every part of the body participates in the one body, so every member of the church participates in the one Lord Jesus Christ. Baptism is a graphic symbol of this real unity of every member with Christ. The same Spirit fills all and works through baptism to break through every human barrier. The true reality of the church has a direct impact upon church life. Every individual Christian has a contribution to make. No one part of the body should feel left out because it is not like another part; for if all were the same, the capacities of the body for fullness of life would be drastically reduced. God himself composes the body to fit his purposes. Bland uniformity of parts would eliminate the very notion of a body; a single body must have many parts in order to work. And furthermore, the body is composed in such a way as to give special care to the weaker, less important, less significant parts — to give greater honor to what is less honorable — so that nothing will divide the harmony of the whole, which is based upon mutual support. Every celebration is shared by all; every concern is carried by all. For the church is the body of Christ, of which every Christian is a particular member. In sum, the Corinthian Christians are to earnestly strive for those gifts that truly contribute to the ongoing life of the community of faith.

Brothers and sisters, to put one's trust in values or agendas or principles instead of in Christ is idolatry. The truth of the gospel alone ignites the flame of human creativity. Do not ask yourself, What can the church do for me? If you approach the matter that way, you will never see past your own needs; you will never discover your own gifts. Ask yourself, What contribution can I make that will help to meet the needs of the church? And then never settle for less than your best effort. If you sing in the choir, sing your heart out; if you teach Sunday school, remember that every word you utter carries the eternal weight of truth; if you help out behind the scenes, show good cheer in every duty; if you serve on the Session, be determined to pour every ounce of wisdom you possess into every decision you make. The presence of God's Spirit in human life channels energy that we never knew we had, stimulates talents that we never before noticed, exacts standards of excellence that we never considered possible. Let us give our best, because of the One to whom we give it.

4. 1 Corinthians 13

We continue today our series of sermons based upon Paul's first letter to the Corinthians. We considered last week the amazing array of gifts that God has showered upon the church through the presence of his Spirit. The body of Christ is composed in such a way that each individual member has a contribution to make, and the whole community receives the benefit when each one gives his or her best effort in the service of Christ. We spoke of the crying need for creativity in the Christian church of the present age, over against the dull ideologies of left and right. In our text for today, Paul radically shifts the topic, the tone, the context, and the purpose of his comments to the church at Corinth. Up until now he has addressed specific questions that they have faced in their life together; now he offers the Corinthians a comprehensive rule by which to judge every question the Christian will face. Paul describes for the church at Corinth, and for all Christians everywhere, the sheer poetry of the Christian life. Brothers and sisters, hear the Word of God.

There is a road for Christian behavior that looks promising, but in fact leads nowhere. Paul's first task is to close off that road at the very point where it begins. The road he closes off is the road of commitment. Paul makes clear that commitment to a cause, however deep, does not lead to Christian discipleship. Perhaps such commitment has given me a golden tongue; perhaps it has inspired me to scale the heights of human wisdom and knowledge; perhaps it has instilled in me a tremendous positive attitude about the world; perhaps it has motivated me to use all my resources to care for the needy; perhaps it has led me to give up my very life for others. Despite all of these impressive achievements, commitment to a cause does not lead to Christ. It has nothing to do with the requirements for Christian discipleship. All of these human attainments mentioned by Paul represent commitment at its deepest possible level; yet such commitment has nothing to do with the Christian life. Paul does not say, "Be more committed"; instead, he says, "Learn to love." Without love, human eloquence is shrill and offensive, acts of kindness and mercy yield no transformation of human character, the genuine humanity of Christian existence has not even been perceived.

It is no surprise that both the religious left and the religious right speak of commitment. They disagree strongly over the causes to which one should be committed; but they agree, just as strongly, that commitment is the heart of Christian faith. And so their preaching and teaching are geared to raising the level of commitment among Christians to its highest form. But both left and right have fallen into the same trap. Commitment never breaks out of the self-enclosed world of human sin. To be committed is to follow the dictates of a particular cause or platform; but real people, with concrete problems and concerns, walk right by unnoticed. Commitment calls for a supreme extension of the self to include the same care for others that we devote to ourselves. But that is to turn discipleship into a form of self-improvement, which it most surely is not. Commitment depends upon a constant influx of reinforcement and inspiration to keep it going; it has no knowledge of the exhilarating joy of discipleship. You cannot respond to the call of the gospel through such commitment; it will get you nowhere, it will only lead you astray. The gospel does not require commitment; it demands a new creation.

Paul starts all over, from the ground up. If commitment leads nowhere, love leads everywhere. Love opens my eyes to the true needs of others; it changes who I am at the most basic level; it guides me through every step of life with the energy of delight and magnanimity. Love is always kind and patient toward others; it does not exact a return for every wrong it receives, but gives every benefit of the doubt it possibly can. Love does not see the accomplishments of others as a source of comparison and jealousy; it sees them as opportunities for praise and congratulation. Love never calls attention to itself; it never announces to others the efforts that make it possible, but instead keeps them hidden in the presence of God alone. Love observes every boundary of decent and fair treatment of others; it is never irritable or petulant; it doesn't keep a perpetual catalogue of the foolish deeds of others, but forgets them as soon as they occur. Love is never happy when injustice is allowed to stand in the world; on the contrary, it rejoices when wrongs are made right. Love does not wax and wane; it is perpetual and charged with vigor at all times. Nothing can diminish it; nothing can disturb its equilibrium; nothing can knock it off course; nothing can bring it to a halt. Love triumphs over the whole world.

Surely the world has changed drastically since Paul wrote these words. The possibilities in human existence have increased dramatically, forcing a constant barrage of decisions never faced in earlier times. The mobility of society has removed a sense of security that could once be taken for granted. The advance of technology has introduced into human life a dynamic of problem-solving that is unique in human history. But the changes have not rendered Paul's message less effective; if anything, they have made it even more spectacular. Christian love is the only way to flourish as a human being in the modern world. Through love, we measure the decisions that we face by the real impact for good that they make, not by the false promises of success they advertise. Through love, we swim through the strong currents of fad and clever packaging; we find dry land, we build a home, and we live our days in the thrill of obedience. Through love, we turn away from solutions that only create fresh problems, that only stir up controversy and conflict; we meet real needs one item at a time, in the service of those we care for. Through love we embrace life, and we never lose our bearings by listening to the propaganda of the age.

Paul makes clear the eternal validity of the rule of love he is communicating to the Corinthian Christians. Some aspects of the Christian life, however important they now are, will one day cease to exist. He

140

has in mind the return of Christ and the final consummation of all things in the kingdom of God. At that point, the divine gift of announcing the future will perish from the earth, because the future will be swallowed up in God's eternal presence. Ecstatic expressions of profound joy will no longer be limited to a few individuals because rapturous exultation will be universal to all humankind. Progress in human understanding will no longer count for anything, because every human being will be filled with all the knowledge of God. A change will come at the end of time; now, in this age, everything is at best partial, incomplete, imperfect; but at the end of time, all things will be enveloped in sheer perfection. The partial will be cast aside. Paul introduces two analogies to press his point. A child has a way of looking at things, a way of expressing things, that is appropriate for youth, but inappropriate for adulthood. The contrast is between the immature and the mature. Or again, if you see an image in a mirror, it is inevitably distorted; nothing can replace viewing an object directly. The contrast is between the indistinct and the distinct. All knowledge in this age is affected by human limitation; but in the eternal future, we shall know God just as fully as he already knows us. Paul's conclusion? Three things will transcend the change that is to come and will carry us over from the present into eternity: faith, hope, and love. And the greatest of these is love.

Brothers and sisters, these are astonishing words. When you love in the present, you are already becoming what you will be in eternity. Despite the radical change in human life that will be ushered in with the second coming of Christ, one thing will not change: the permanence of love in the definition of human character. In a changing world, love shows you where to find eternal happiness. In an uncertain age, love clarifies the true sources of eternal joy. In a time of boundless opportunity, love illuminates the narrow paths of eternal abundance. Love orders aright the priorities of living, showing you the difference between short-term advantage and long-term fulfillment. Love stretches the range of vision to a distant horizon, molds the plans of the present to the dreams of the future, expands the scope of human endeavor to the outer limit. As you follow the lead of love, you travel a path that will not end with your death. It leads from time to eternity, from this age to the next, from passing moments to the eternal Now. Follow where it leads, follow it until the end; for the end is the true beginning.

5. 1 Corinthians 15:1-34

We conclude today our series of sermons based upon Paul's first letter to the Corinthians. As we have seen, this letter addresses a variety of topics raised for Paul by the local situation in the church at Corinth. He speaks to each one in turn, sometimes with cautious advice, sometimes with bold affirmation, sometimes with strident warning. But does the book simply address Christian ethics? Is there not a broader theological perspective that guides the whole? The answer to these questions is contained in the fifteenth chapter. The resurrection of Christ and the fervent Christian expectation of redemption are the hidden ground for every item of reflection that the book contains. The beginning and the middle are contained in the end; and the end to which all things move is the risen Lord. Brothers and sisters, hear the Word of God.

Apostolic testimony means the gospel; that is what the apostles are commissioned to preach, that is what Christians are summoned to embrace. Paul's letter teaches the gospel, and it is the same gospel he had already preached in Corinth in person. The gospel is not an arcane password; the church is not a secret society with a hidden agenda. The gospel has been made known to the whole world, and it is contained in the traditional teaching of the church. The church at Corinth has inherited and treasured that tradition; the message it encompasses contains their eternal salvation. Indeed, Paul reminds them of their obligation to remember that message if they hope to retain a living faith. Paul is the teacher of the Corinthians; but he himself was first a student who learned the gospel that he now teaches. To proclaim what he has learned is the highest priority of his existence. What is the gospel? That Christ died for the sins of humankind and rose again, and that he appeared to many witnesses, including last of all Paul himself. Paul refers to himself as "one untimely born," a miscarriage, which may be a name his enemies commonly used of him. Paul freely admits that he is the johnny-come-lately among the apostles — a complete nobody. Nothing but the grace of God turned a persecutor of the church into its most ardent builder. But he also exudes the quiet self-confidence of one who is doing exactly what he is told to do, no more and no less, and even points out that the fruits of his work outdistance by far any other apostle. His work is God's gift, not human achievement. The focus is not on

142

the one who preaches but on what is preached, with the goal of eager faith among all.

At times it is helpful to consider that we who believe in the gospel are not alone. We are here today because we know, at every level of our existence, that the salvation freely offered in Christ is the only hope for our eternal future. We are here because we are sinners, who trust in the mercy of God through the death of his Son and his resurrection from the dead. We profess faith in Jesus Christ as Lord and Savior. Recall for a moment that there are people like us in every country throughout the world. There are people like us of every race, every class, every occupation, every variety of human circumstance, the world over. If we ask them: "Why do you live?" they will answer, as we would, "Because Jesus Christ is my hope for tomorrow." If we ask them: "What do you want out of life?" they will answer, as we would, "That I do my best to follow the ways of Christ every day of my life." They may speak a different language; they may or may not know anything of the comforts and conveniences that we take for granted; they may have obligations that we never dreamed of and troubles that we have never faced; but they are our brothers and sisters in one hope, one faith, one gospel.

Paul now enters a phase of his argument that modern critical scholarship has been able to illuminate considerably. It was once thought that Paul was attacking those in Corinth who simply denied that the resurrection will ever occur. Such a denial is certainly a prominent feature of modern times, and we will return to it in a moment. However, aspects of Paul's approach are unintelligible if that was the issue he was facing. Instead, it is now clear that he was facing opponents who believed that the general resurrection had already occurred. "There is no resurrection" represents these opponents' claim that there is no longer any need for a resurrection, because it has already happened. And that Paul radically denies. What Christians mean by the resurrection to come is focused upon the person of Christ. Christ has already been raised in glory, and the Christian expectation of an eternal future is measured by his risen identity. There is most assuredly a resurrection still to come, for the Christian hope is to be forever in the presence of the Lord. Without that hope there is no point to preaching, to faith, to life itself. If Christ has not been raised to eternal glory, then Christians are liars, their hopes for forgiveness are empty wishes, their confidence in an eternal future for those they love is misplaced. But in fact, Jesus Christ is already risen from the dead, the first of all to follow who belong to him.

The errors of modernity are different from the errors of antiquity, but the same gospel conquers both. Modernity is convinced that it has mastered the secret of time. It looks backward and sees the rise and fall of nations. It looks forward and calculates the possibilities that lie ahead. And between the past and the future, it draws a straight line through the present. Conservatives look back to the past along that line, and liberals look ahead, but the same line connects both. History is perceived as an open system of linear movement from the past to the future. But the Christian understanding of time moves in a very different direction. We look backward, and we see the person of Christ, through whom all things were made. We look ahead, and we see the return of Christ, toward whom all things move. The sovereign purpose of Christ rules the nations of the world in hidden mystery, beyond the gaze of human inspection and comprehension. The activity of Christ in the life of the individual is filled with surprise and incredible adventure beyond any human prediction. History is a closed system; Jesus Christ is the alpha and the omega, the beginning and the end. Yet history contains an unending abundance of unexpected blessings, impossible wonders, miraculous loves.

Paul focuses in upon the final return of Christ. Death entered the human race with the sin of Adam, and it is universal to all; so also is the resurrection universal to all through the person of Christ. But there is a proper order: Christ is the first-fruits of the eternal future, to be followed by all others at his second coming. The return of Christ is not a new phase of human history; it is the end of all history, when the rule of Christ over the entire universe will be openly visible to all. His rule is already real, yet it must still accomplish the ultimate destruction of evil. Of all the harms that afflict humankind the very worst is death. The return of Christ will abolish death forever. God has already placed the whole of reality under the sovereign control of Christ, and his return will bring to fulfillment the purpose for which he exercises that control. Paul is insistent that the Christians in Corinth not lose sight of the second coming. Without it, cherished hopes for family and friends who have died are false hopes. Without it, the whole point of enduring the many trials of daily living is lost completely. Paul makes sure that they understand just how much his own ministry has cost him personally. If there is no return of Christ, what good does it do to struggle against the unscrupulous deeds of wicked persons? It would be much easier simply to go along with the crowd. Paul makes sure that they see that the expected return of Christ impinges directly upon the way they live everyday life. Keeping company with the wrong crowd always rubs off in the worst way. It is time for them to come to their senses and stop doing what they know is wrong. Some of them are ignorant of God, and they should not be proud of that fact.

Brothers and sisters, let us be clear about the hope that we cherish in our hearts as our deepest joy. As we, the Christian church in all the earth, gather together around the Lord's table, what future do we celebrate? We believe in the return of Jesus Christ as the one hope of the whole world. We are not misled by those who tell us that our hope is a delusion. We are not misled by those who try to predict for us what will appear in tomorrow's newspaper. We, the Christian church of all denominations, trust, with our very lives and every good thing that they contain, that our Lord will come again to take us to himself for all eternity. We feed on his body here today, because we yearn for his eternal presence; we partake of his blood, because we relish his eternal love. The promise of Christ to come again for our salvation will see us through every sleepless night, no matter how troubling; every trial of adversity, no matter how difficult; every pain to body and soul, no matter how agonizing. Christ will come again: the promise fills the earth with exultation.

XII

PSALM 131

The Christian faith is not just one mode of authentic human living among others. On the contrary, the gospel encompasses the true measure of all genuine humanity. Nothing human is alien to the gospel's concerns; nothing characteristic of human experience is left untouched by its witness. Nowhere is this dimension of the church's proclamation more explicitly spelled out than in the Psalms. Like a physician examining a patient, like a scientist scrutinizing a new specimen, like a musician analyzing a score, the Psalter lays bear every facet of human existence for those who labor with its contents. The Psalms are the laboratory of human life, where the experiment of living is tested and refined. Above all else, written over the entire Psalter is the clear invitation: if you would know God, you must know yourself. Brothers and sisters, hear the Word of God.

Psalm 131 is one of the shortest psalms in the Bible, but it contains a wondrous image of human life under the grace of God. The psalm is ascribed to David, which immediately places its message in the context of the life of this member of the community of faith. David confesses that he has learned an astonishing lesson about the life of obedience. He has learned not to allow his concerns in life to outstrip his capacity to carry them out. To be arrogant is to pretend responsibility for what in fact is well beyond one's resources. To be vain is to pretend that one's vision extends beyond the capacity of the eye to focus properly. To go astray is to occupy oneself with issues in life that are beyond

146

one's comprehension and that transcend the limits of one's duties. All of these, David admits to God, he has now realized are a major mistake in the search for the good life.

Surely one of the greatest temptations human beings face is the temptation to assume responsibility for aspects of the world that are beyond the divinely ordained limits of our tasks in life. We apply the gifts that we have received to the concrete jobs we have been commissioned to perform. By the mercy of God, we succeed; and that is when temptation lurks and disaster threatens. For the next step commonly taken is to assume that our success is a license to go beyond the limits set by God's commandments, applying our gifts to a purpose contrary to the divine will. Our intentions may be profoundly honorable and genuine, but the only possible outcome of such activity is utter misery for ourselves and others. Human pride has prompted us to apply a divine gift outside the realm of God's command. We try to help, and we end up causing only trouble; we try to do good, and we leave others worse off than before. We turn the gift of life into endless weary frustration, which steals away the pleasure of God's presence. It is essential to recognize this pattern before it sets in and to bring it to a halt. God's gifts are given for his purposes, and not for ours; any confusion on this point will bring certain ruin.

And now David introduces his lovely image, to expand upon the positive side of his lesson in life. In stark contrast to the habit of overreaching his limits, David has learned an approach to life that yields composure and calm at all times. Genuine human existence is like a small child lying contentedly in the lap of his mother. The image is clear and profoundly forceful. To live is to enjoy God with unbounded exuberance and to savor the good things that he has brought into one's daily life. The contrast could not be greater than with the one who frantically exceeds the limits of life, losing all sense of the sheer pleasure of being alive in God's world and under the luxurious hand of God's care. The arrogance of inflated self-importance has given way to the sheer delight of being a creature. The posturing of human manipulation has given way to the gracious reserve of duty fulfilled. The incessant worry of mistaken self-admiration has given way to enjoyment of the utter grandeur of everyday life in the kingdom of God.

Why do we exist? For what purpose has God placed us in the world that he fashioned from nothing as a wonderland for human endeavor?

He has put us here to obey his commandments. No human being can ever ignore those commandments and remain human. But our psalm for today emphasizes the opposite point, which is also true: no human being can add to those commandments and remain the creature God intends us to be. To add to God's commandments is to play God, a role at which we are doomed to fail. To obey them is to let God be God, and that brings the greatest satisfaction of life known to humankind. This realization affects daily life at the most intimate level. There is no longer any need to fret about what is beyond my ability to control or my power to influence; I now have the glory of time to understand what I before scarcely noticed. There is no longer any need to waste effort bringing to pass what in fact is a passing distraction. I now have the freedom to act and the incredible confidence that my activity goes toward the real accomplishment of a goal. There is no longer cause for panic, as if my control over events is what guarantees my survival. I now have the luxury to appreciate every single item of brilliant splendor that God shows to me in his glorious creation. He hovers over his own, with passionate desire to display his marvelous love.

Let us briefly inspect a single dimension of the joy of obedience more closely. As we have said, every human being is given by God certain obligations to fulfill, regardless of the circumstances. Those obligations are clearly spelled out in Scripture and summarized in the Ten Commandments. Ultimately, our obligation to fulfill them is not to other human beings, but to God himself, the Lord of all life. But Scripture also preserves a rich background of human personality that adds color and form to the tapestry of creation. You know best where your limits lie; you know best how far your gifts extend; you know best where your true abilities lead. Every human being is tugged and pulled this way and that by the good intentions of others. But it is up to you to say no, politely but firmly, when you know the direction suggested is the wrong one to take. If you say yes, you invite calamity for yourself and others and have no one to blame but yourself. Say no, and make it stick; it is neither safe nor wise to go beyond God's revealed will.

The brief psalm ends with a simple declaration of hope. Israel's expectation for the future is always oriented toward the living person of God. At no time in human life is hope rendered obsolete; hope embraces all of life and transcends time into eternity. The present psalm does not comment further, but it is well to hear its voice in the chorus of hope that springs from the witness of Scripture. Nowhere does the Bible deny the real hardships of life; nowhere does it trivialize human pain and suffering; nowhere does it seek to conceal the desperation often contained in human circumstances. And yet time and again it proclaims, there is always hope. The reason for that perpetual assurance concerning the future is that the chain of causality is subordinate to the creativity of God. God is not limited by the circumstances of the present in bringing the future to pass. Where resources fail, God creates new resources from nothing; where human stamina weakens, God brings into being fresh sources of strength and support that quicken weary steps and stiffen faltering resolve. But how long, we might ask? How long will God bring the future into being beyond the horizons of the present? Here, a passage from the prophet Hosea is helpful, especially since it uses the same image of childhood employed by our psalm. Because the people of Israel are the children of God, God is compelled to tell them: "How can I give you up, O Ephraim! How can I hand you over, O Israel! . . . My heart recoils within me. . . . I will not execute my fierce anger; . . . for I am God . . . and I will not come to destroy" (Hosea 11:8-9). How can God ever abandon the child whom he loves so intensely? It cannot and will not happen. Hope is as eternal as God's undying love.

Brothers and sisters, the present psalm contains a mystery of life that is beyond rational calculation and yet governs human affairs with absolute certainty. If you try to do more than you can in life, you will end up doing less than you should. But if you do only what you should, you will accomplish more than you ever dreamed. There is no way to unravel the threads of this mystery. Every effort to straighten out its contents will automatically distort its spectacular truth. The ground of the mystery is God's everlasting compassion. He wants two things from your life: he wants you to recognize and to admit by the way you live that you are his creature, and not your own master; and he wants you to succeed beyond any possible wish you have ever cherished. You cannot have one without the other. You cannot live as your own master and succeed in life. But the opposite is also true: you cannot fail to have the second, if you follow the first. God's infinite desire is to bring nothing but inexhaustible treasures of joy into the lives of his children. You cannot fail, because the Lord of heaven and earth will most surely bring it to pass.

XIII

FROM PROVERBS

1. Proverbs 1:1-9

We begin today a series of sermons based upon the book of Proverbs. The Old Testament is divided into three broad sections: the Law, the Prophets, and the Writings. Both the Law and the Prophets have a clear theological profile, and for generations Christian proclamation has followed along general lines clearly perceived by the church. But the Writings, which include the wisdom books such as Job, Ecclesiastes, and Proverbs, are a fresh field for the cultivation of Christian witness. Only recently in church scholarship have certain features of these books come sharply into focus. The book of Proverbs is the centerpiece of the wisdom books of the Old Testament. The Reformation era once heard resounding notes of profound challenge from this sacred text. Can the church in our time rediscover the explosive power of wisdom, which reaches down into every corner of creation? Brothers and sisters, hear the Word of God.

The opening passage of the book of Proverbs is a prologue for the whole book, and the first verse is a superscription explaining the true context for its appropriation. The book is ascribed to Solomon, the son of David, who reigned as king over Israel. Several comments are in order about this brief verse. First, the concept of authorship being employed here is only loosely related to the modern notion of writing a book. Proverbs itself contains several statements about different authors of various portions of the book. Yet, despite the disparate origins, the book as a whole is assigned to Solomon. Remember that Solomon is described in 1 Kings as one who devoted his whole life to the acquisition of wisdom. He searched all things in creation — plants and animals, human society, interpersonal relations, government, economics, and so forth. His sources were cosmopolitan; his reputation was international. Recall the visit of the queen of Sheba, who was amazed at what he had learned. That earnest and refined effort of Solomon to discern the ways of God in all features of life establishes the comprehensive theme for the book that bears his name. What is contained in this book is wisdom, which is the one source of right understanding of the created universe.

How does this opening verse affect the way we approach the book of Proverbs in the Christian church today? Our first conclusion is that the wisdom books of the Old Testament are not to be squeezed into the mold of the Law and the Prophets. The Law has one function, and the Prophets another; but the wisdom books have still another, and they must be heard on their own terms. There are questions in the Christian life that cannot be answered simply yes or no. These questions call for seasoned reflection, not simplistic bombast; for sustained analysis, not knee-jerk reaction; for total concentration, not empty slogans. The Proverbs give us a vigorous stimulus to such reflection, but everything rests upon finding just the right situation in human life to illuminate their content. Second, the wisdom books are the one portion of the canon of Scripture that openly invites comparison with extrabiblical material. The Christian church has always held that the tools of culture are necessary to the right understanding of Scripture. Nowhere is this more evident than in the exposition of the wisdom books, which requires all the resources at one's disposal. And third, the book of Proverbs makes it clear that the acquisition of wisdom, as the highest priority of human existence, is itself a sheer paradox. On the one hand, wisdom is an active force in all creation. It not only orders the affairs of humankind and the natural world but also summons every human being to grasp its message. In Proverbs 8, wisdom is personified as a resplendent woman who was present when the world was created and who calls from every street corner to every human being. Wisdom is a gift, not an achievement. On the other hand, wisdom cannot be received without the highest human exertion. If you really want it, it is up to you to undertake the search for it.

The prologue continues by describing what is to be found in the proverbs to follow. Here is where a genuine comprehension of human life in the mystery of creation can be attained. Here is where personal discipline in the school of wisdom can be engaged. Here is where the true explanations of reality itself can be penetrated by the human mind. The vocabulary of the prologue shows that much more is at stake than ethics, though right behavior is certainly involved. Here the patterns of truth are recognized against the backdrop of human events. Those patterns are not only features of the real world; they are also a guide to the best forms of human action: honesty, fairness, concern for the marginalized. Who will benefit from a study of wisdom in the sayings of this book? A person who has trouble deciding which advice should be accepted will gain prudence, the ability to choose the right path from competing alternatives. The young person, who has not yet had time to experience all the marvels of existence, will learn what to look for and how to plan appropriately. Even experienced persons of deep knowledge will add to their mastery of human affairs. The cycle of wisdom never ends, bringing greater insight to those who know best where to find it. In short, the purpose of the book of Proverbs is to train the mind to see the enigma of creation, which is reflected in the cadences of these figurative sayings. Live by these sayings, and the blessing of creation is opened up.

The service of Christ does not take place in an alien environment, devoid of his purpose. Rather, the astonishing truth is that all forces of social and natural life have their rightful place in the rule of Christ over the vast universe that he brought into being. Christian discipleship is not a withdrawal from the world. We live in a time of human history when massive amounts of time and money are spent providing mechanisms of escape. The drug culture is certainly the most lethal and destructive form of such escape, but it is not the only one. There are also the many artificial environments that close people off from the world of nature, the genres of entertainment that trade on overstimulation at the cost of contact with the real world, and the many applications of technology toward the manufacture of an alternative time and space. As Christians, we can only recognize this burst of escapism as a sad loss for humankind, especially because we love the beauty of the world that God has made. We relish the plants and animals, which are our neighbors in the grand system of living creatures; we cherish the rhythm of time in the seasons of life; we take delight in the interaction of human beings in the structures of society. We do not want to escape; why should we escape that which we enjoy so much? Instead, we want to learn how best to derive from the world every benefit of joy that it will give us. To escape is the way of the fool; to learn is the way of the wise.

The prologue lays down a fundamental rule for all progress in the study of wisdom. Wisdom begins and ends with the fear of God. The issue in the book of Proverbs is not one of legalistic adherence to stated rules. Something far broader and more wholistic is at stake. The human capacity to understand the world rightly is grounded in a basic loyalty to God that spans all regions of human life. That loyalty is thoroughly practical. All of human experience must be captivated by devotion to God, if proper knowledge of the created order is to be found. There is no way to split apart aspects of human existence and still succeed in the search for understanding; no one can grasp with the mind what is ignored in one's deeds; no one can act rightly in an arena of life that is not thoughtfully examined; no one can make progress in comprehension if one's heart is really elsewhere. The whole person must be employed in the pursuit of understanding; then, and only then, is the joy of discovery granted by the wisdom of God. The ignorant are empty-headed because they do not give God his due; they disdain the discipline that he enjoins upon them and so lose their grip on the good life. The words of this book are words of life, passed along from a parent to a child. To do them is to inherit a brilliant wreath of human accomplishment; to embrace them is to wear wisdom around one's neck like a sparkling pendant.

Brothers and sisters, the purpose of Jesus Christ for our good in life is built into the very structure of reality. We do not need to fear the basic order of the universe, for it is derived from the mind of Christ. Instead of fear, there is sheer wonder. What makes the difference between successes and failures, when all other things seem to be equal? How does one explain the tendency of human beings to act against their own self-interest? When is the right time to act, and where is one to concentrate what energy one has to give? How can we tell what will bring us real happiness in life, and what will turn out in the end to be a drain on our joy? Christ does not want us to make our way through life without full understanding of the answers to such questions. He has given us the book of Proverbs to make those answers clear. But he also refuses to sell those answers cheaply. They can only be paid for by total exertion of life above every earthly distraction; for they contain glorious rapture above every earthly satisfaction.

2. Proverbs 16:9

We continue today our series of sermons based upon the book of Proverbs. We began last week by considering the prologue to the book, which describes the theological role of wisdom in the good life. The human person is created by God to live with skill and happiness in the world that God has made for human fulfillment. Wisdom is first of all the very characteristic of reality itself, which operates according to an order established by God for human protection and beatitude. But wisdom is also the gift of recognizing that order and adjusting one's life to take full advantage of it. If wisdom is violated, one will pay the price; but if wisdom is sought and embraced in the totality of one's existence, then the good that exists in creation will redound to one's own benefit. God wills above all else human contentment and development; through the sayings of this book, he shows the eager reader how to find both in supreme abundance. We consider today the first of three proverbs; brothers and sisters, hear the Word of God.

"A man's mind plans his way: but the LORD directs his steps." Like most of the proverbs in the Old Testament, the form of this proverb is a couplet: a single saying with two parallel parts that need to be measured against one another. The form and content of wisdom are closely interrelated; there is an inherent complexity to the divine order that cannot be grasped by an inflexible moralism. Oftentimes the couplet is a simple contrast; other times the second part augments the first; still other times the two parts give different dimensions of the same created process. Needless to say, one of the great challenges to the study of Proverbs is to handle correctly the shades of meaning contained in the

154

couplet form. Our proverb for today does not set forth a right way and a wrong way; nor does it show two parts of the whole or two different ways to the same goal. Rather, it describes two different ways of looking at the same progression of human life. The first way is the human perspective; the second is the divine perspective. Neither perspective cancels out the other, for both are legitimate; and yet neither can be fully understood without the other.

"A man's mind plans his way." Human beings make plans. Human beings construct projects in life that guide their endeavors. The point is not that human beings have thereby acted wickedly; this proverb is not an attempt to censure thoughtful designs for the future as inherently impious. Rather, it begins with a simple observation about the way responsible people act in the world. They do what they can to plan ahead. But then suddenly something completely unexpected intervenes. Something happens that lifts the affairs of human life completely out of the hands of the one who has formulated such a careful strategy. Again, the proverb is not blaming the person; it is not saying, "you should have known what was coming and prepared accordingly." Instead, it is observing a limit to all human action. Something happens that was not foreseen, because it could not be foreseen. It is not a question of what is not known in advance but should have been known; it is a question of what is not known in advance and can never be known. The limit that human life is encountering is one of absolute mystery.

But the essential point of the proverb is not reached until the second part of the couplet is taken into account. Where does that limit come from? How is a person to cope with it? "But the LORD directs his steps." This proverb is not talking about the well-known limitation of human vision concerning the future. "No one knows what will happen tomorrow": that is a truism hardly worth the time to consider. The reflection of the wise takes a different direction. The correct observation is that God himself intervenes in human life, to protect individuals from their own well-laid plans. The limit is not one of human finitude; the limit is one of unpredictable divine intervention. God himself is the limit upon all human design. There is not one direct line from the inception of a life project to its fulfillment. The mystery of God intersects that line and fashions a new direction for human life. The new direction is not shaky or uncertain; on the contrary, the path is clearly marked by God and easily followed. The destination is not vague or undesirable; in fact, God himself has now set a new goal for human achievement and shown exactly how to get there.

Now, how do we adjust the balance between these two parts of the proverb? The astonishing conclusion is that a human being is far better off not having complete control over the decisions of life. Human beings are fortunate indeed that they are not the captives of their own plans in life. This is not to condemn human planning per se; nor is it to try out a new theology of human action and divine response. It is to point to a hidden dimension of human experience that in the end turns out to be the salvation of human happiness. God sees ahead where human plans lead to trouble; he sees where disaster is about to strike, and he intervenes to turn that disaster into fresh possibility for the future. He actively takes over the control of human affairs, beyond any human choice; and he starts the life of a person all over again with infinite benefit because of the changes that have occurred.

Now, what does this proverb mean for the way we live our lives? The lesson is not: "Do not make too many plans or you will be disappointed." The lesson is not: "No one can know the future, so you'd better limit your attention to the present." The lesson is far more profound. Every serious Christian makes plans in life. No attempt is made by this proverb to condemn that activity. But there will come times in your life when your plans will suddenly evaporate before your very eyes. Factors may come into play that you had no way of knowing beforehand. Circumstances may drastically change that gave every appearance of remaining stable. What will you do? You could dig in your heels and follow your plans to the bitter end, despite the fact that the conditions have radically changed. Needless to say, you will not reach the goal you intend. Or you could panic and turn inward, as if the change in your life has only confirmed your worst suspicions about the hostility of the universe. Human beings cannot see ahead, you might reason, and reality will not cooperate, and so we are all doomed to fail. Again, you may convince yourself, but you will not grow in wisdom. The limitation of human life is not a lesson about the futility of human effort, but about the magnificence of God.

So, what will you do? If your plans are falling apart around you, consider what God might be telling you. Perhaps the path you were following does not lead to the dreams you cherish most. Perhaps the road you were taking could never make possible the great contribution you hope to make with the talents you've been given. However difficult it is to give up our plans, we know that God knows what will work for our good better than we do. Leave behind the plans of the past, however inviting they may have been, and trust that God will show you a better way. Take the steps that he lays out before you, and never again will you doubt the goodness of life in the world of creation.

Brothers and sisters, we all do our best, and we can ask no more. But the fact is that there is One who knows far better than we do the most intimate secrets of our existence. He knows where we will flourish, and he plants us right there. He knows where our horizons will expand, and he takes us right there. He knows how to draw from us a level of productivity and a degree of excellence that we never thought possible, and he shows us precisely how to do it. Walk in the path of the Lord; you can be sure that the finest dreams of human desire lie fulfilled at the end of that path.

3. Proverbs 19:14

We continue today our series of sermons based upon the book of Proverbs. Last week, we reflected upon the characteristic form of the proverbs, the couplet. We noticed the inherent subtlety in the very form of proverbial wisdom and the complexity of thought required to explore the various dimensions of reality. We spoke of the reasonable task of making plans, which is involved in all mature human behavior. But we also recognized the mystery of divine action, which seizes hold of human plans unexpectedly and alters the human future toward its true destiny. To be guided by God through the many changes of life is the tremendous blessing of the wise. Beyond all human calculation, God establishes human existence in motion toward perfect completion. Let us consider today the second of our three proverbs. Brothers and sisters, hear the Word of God.

Once again, the form of our proverb is a couplet, and once again the challenge is to weigh carefully the balance between the two parts. "House and property are inherited from fathers." This is not a moral observation but a social one. No effort is made to justify the economic system of ancient times, nor to condemn it; rather, the point is that this is the way things happen. A young man would reach an age when he was ready to make a start in life. Almost everyone could count on help from one's family to get going. It might be a large inheritance, or it might be small; but usually sons moved into an active adult life by receiving a portion of the family holdings to manage. We can make a similar observation today, but we would make it somewhat differently because of the differences between a modern economy and an ancient one. Today we would probably say to our sons and daughters: "A good education will get you a good job." "If you finish school, and show a little initiative, you can find a way to make a living." Again, the issue is not a matter of social ethics, but simply a sociological constant.

"But a sensible wife is from the Lord." Here, there is very little need to worry about the difference between ancient times and our own. Somehow, the wise observation of the sages of Israel leaps right off the page into contemporary times. The gist of the saying is this: Who can possibly know ahead of time how the decision of marriage will work out? So much in life is riding upon this one choice of wife or husband; who can possibly take credit for making the right one? One surely has to admit that a good marriage is a gift from God, pure and simple. Elsewhere in the book of Proverbs, the qualities of an ideal wife are treated at length, and they clearly shatter the images of femininity common throughout antiquity. A good wife is the greatest gift ever received; her advice is rock solid, her habits are thrifty and enterprising, her household lives with supreme joy and beauty. She takes care of the needs of the disadvantaged, she contributes to human society through her skill and knowledge, she spreads affirmation and graciousness wherever she goes. She begins the day with eagerness and ends it with self-confidence; all around her are warmed by her glow and cheered on by the kindness in her voice. Her faith fills life itself with love and creativity. Such a woman only God can grant to human happiness.

Now let us ask, what mystery of human living is concealed between the lines of this ancient proverb? What pattern of human experience were the sages of Israel seeking to discern and communicate? Some aspects of human life can pretty much be counted on as routine and ordinary. Some people may have more in life, others may have less; but nowadays society contains various mechanisms that attempt to meet the basic needs of most people. But there are other aspects of life that no human being can count on as automatic; and in fact it is these aspects that make life worth living. There is no way to guarantee that one will have these blessings, no way to assure in advance that one's decisions will lead to them. Indeed, it is mostly in looking back that one realizes that one has had them all along. The source of those blessings is God alone. He makes life worth living by filling the routine with unbounded pleasure. The wise know just how good the life they have been given truly is, and they know exactly where the credit is due.

Many of you know firsthand the God-given joys of a loving marriage. Think back for a moment to the day you said yes to your husband or wife. There is no way you could possibly have known at that time the ups and downs your life together would have in the years ahead. There is no way you could have known for sure that standing next to you was the one person on this earth who would give you every support and encouragement one human being can give to another, through a thousand variations of life's adventures. You could not have known for sure that you were about to begin life with the greatest enticement to all your desires, the truest answer to all your dreams. You could have no idea of the great comfort you would receive from their affection and the overwhelming benefit you would derive from their counsel. The treasure of delight that you have received from your marriage did not just happen. God himself steps into the picture and transforms the ordinary decisions of life into a fountain of unending bliss.

The example supplied by the proverb still applies directly; yet it also opens a window upon the fresh air of divine generosity. It is one thing to bring home a paycheck every month, but it is quite another to be captivated by a calling. Whether it is as a banker, a farmer, a nurse, a teacher, a business owner, or something else, a calling in life is anything but routine. When you wake up in the morning, your first thoughts are of how you can do your best today, because you care infinitely about the quality of your work. You sweat the details, because you know that the people you serve deserve the best effort that you can give them. You do not work to buy time for leisure; you work because you cannot imagine your life spent any other way than engaging in the tasks your vocation brings along. You love those tasks and cherish every moment of time you spend doing them. You are not simply employed; you are exercising a calling. Where does such a calling come from? How does it come about that some human beings suddenly find themselves pouring every ounce of energy they can summon into doing exactly what they enjoy most, and thus bringing the highest possible degree of gain into the lives of others? There is no way that any one human being can calculate all these factors. A calling in life is another of those divine gifts that turn daily living into the richest form of creaturely satisfaction.

Again, everyone ends up living in one place or another. Perhaps a job determines where we go, or family connections, or regional preferences; but one way or another, people find themselves located in a particular spot on this earth. But it is quite another matter to find a home. When you are truly at home, you not only know the names of your next-door neighbors; you know the people of your town and take an active interest in their daily welfare. You begin to learn the special strengths that different people bring to the life of the community. You begin to appreciate the fascinating mesh of human personality, which provides a unique place for every talent under the sun. You hurt when your town hurts; you are exhilarated when it succeeds. You are proud of its achievements when the sons and daughters of your community make good in the wider world. You are amazed at the burst of vitality that pulsates from the core and radiates throughout the whole. You have found a home. How did you find your way there? No human being has so great a grasp of the geography of this earth as to find a place called home. The truth of the matter is, it found you. Perhaps it was while you were looking, perhaps you had no idea what you had missed. To be home is a cherished divine gift that descends from heaven above straight down to the earth beneath. The wise know their way to its doorstep.

And finally, brothers and sisters, it is helpful to remind ourselves, now and again, that we are not the first generation to face difficult times. We have been given a heritage, and that heritage is no stranger to struggle through periods of hardship. Those who have come before us have gladly endured incredible inconveniences and astonishing heartbreaks because they knew in the depths of their being that they were doing what God had given them to do. In the final analysis, what else truly matters? They mustered up astonishing resourcefulness to accomplish their given duties with meager supplies because they realized that the future itself was theirs to seize. How can we ever turn back? They reached their goals in life, and rested from their labors, and inherited a crown of eternal glory. How can we ever strive for anything less?

4. Proverbs 20:12

We conclude today our series of sermons based upon the book of Proverbs. Last week, we reflected upon those gifts in life which no amount of human cleverness can either predict or guarantee. The wisdom of God meets the deepest needs of human beings far beyond our own capacity to identify and assess those needs. Some aspects of life we can count on as commonplace; but God breaks through the normal course of events and turns the ordinary paths of life into journeys of joy and discovery. A marriage becomes the perfect bond of human happiness and fulfillment, completing what is lacking, adding pleasure to pleasure in everyday existence. A job is fashioned into a life calling, which challenges the best in us and repays every effort with fresh growth. A living space is transformed into a home, which grounds our every achievement and brings the cheer of life to ordinary day-to-day living. A heritage stands behind our every thought and word — a heritage so noble as to inspire the highest reach of our endeavors, and so wondrous as to sustain us through the lowest moments of the struggle of faith. Let us consider today the last of our short series of proverbs. Brothers and sisters, hear the Word of God.

"The hearing ear and the seeing eye, the LORD has made them both." This time the couplet form is not used to paint a contrast, or to trace the outline of an enigma; this time it is used to show an intimate connection between a facet of human experience and its divine origin. The proverb discloses the relationship between human perception and divine creativity. The purpose of the proverb is not to argue a theological point about the nature of God or the nature of humankind. Instead, the proverb is trying to make clear to the reader how a certain human

161

activity is the direct result of divine presence in creation. What is that activity? Human beings not only have the capacity to learn; they actively go out into the world in search of knowledge. The eye sees, the ear hears. Human life as a whole is a process of education. To acquire understanding is not a peripheral concern of humanity, carried out at the edges of human experience; in fact, the human person is well structured to investigate the order of creation. The Hebrew idiom of the proverb emphasizes that human beings are amply gifted with a variety of sensors for discerning the form and dimensions of wisdom. Human beings live to learn.

But what is the connection between that activity of learning and the divine presence? To learn is to fulfill the divinely ordained purpose of creaturely life. When human beings acquire fresh comprehension of the way of things in the world, they are not engaging in an exertion foreign to the divine will. They are living out the divine mandate, built into the very substance of human personhood. Human beings are not placed on the earth with such astonishing capacities only to use them frivolously or to let them lie dormant. Laziness and distraction are inherently foolish, because the Creator himself endowed humankind with organs of perception and cognition that are meant to be used. Human beings are responsible to God for the way they use the abilities he has blended into their composition. God wants persons to grasp the underlying connection between cause and effect; to see through the surface confusion of events and recognize the patterns of behavior that emerge; to notice the gap between intention and execution, and the successful bridging of that gap. God created human beings to learn. Human ingenuity in the acquisition of knowledge is the true fulfillment of created potential.

As always, a good proverb contains a world of insight, waiting to be explored. First we must note this comprehensive formulation: we can learn the will of God for human life only by doing it. All genuine knowledge of God is inherently pragmatic. We cannot stand aloof from the world of creation and expect to derive from it the benefits that God has placed there for our enjoyment and enrichment. Our very being is constituted by God in such a way that the best things in life come only once we reach out and grab hold of them. What does this mean for daily Christian experience? The most precious divine gifts are always staring us right in the face. The common mistake is to live ordinary life with the mind turned off and the senses numbed, only to rouse them into action through some form of escape. The result is that the whole person is not engaged in living, and therefore the beauty of creation is ignored. Cherish everyday existence, and it will feed the whole person with perpetual nourishment.

Second, the correct posture of all genuine discipleship is receptivity to the new. Learning is by definition a matter of exploration and discovery. We learn because we want to know what we do not understand; we increase our awareness because we wish to take account of what we had not noticed before. Curiosity and faith go hand in hand. God did not put us in the world with every item of creation already understood, every truth of his will already processed. Instead, he put us here with all the tools of analysis we need to chart the intricate designs of his universe. There are times when even the most established features of our understanding must yield to greater insight; when ideas strongly supported by custom and influence must fall before the onslaught of truth; when habits from the immemorial past of our lives must be left behind for the passion of new life. If we cling to the old when the new has come, we inevitably miss the events of God's eternal kingdom. If we seize the opportunity that the new brings, we are never the same again.

Third, education in the will of God for human welfare is wholistic and flexible. It is wholistic because every aspect of creation is taken into account. Individual human action is set against the backdrop of the changing times of human society; accurate description of human behavior is interlaced with norms of fairness and honesty; proper weight is assigned to common understanding and inherited usage. We can learn nothing at all if we close our minds to even one aspect of the goodness of life in God's universe. However small it may appear, it will trip us up and leave us straggling behind. Wisdom is all or nothing, because God himself fills the universe with his glory. It is flexible, because the universe itself is a living organism under the divine ordering. Day to day brings fresh experience to ponder; week to week brings new fields of information to cultivate and harvest; season to season shines the light of discovery upon different areas of divine purpose.

Fourth, to learn the divine wisdom that makes human life human is profoundly constant. The wisdom of God is with us when we wake up in the morning, ready to start a new day with enthusiasm for the tasks that lie ahead. It walks us through difficult decisions, conflicting priorities, clashing opinions, and social turmoil; it straightens out what is crooked, shades in what is one-dimensional, adjusts to perfect pitch what is out of tune. It accompanies us in work and play, in times with family and friends, in common life and time alone; and it eases into place mature familiarity with what is best for human happiness in all circumstances. It starts alongside us when we are young, showing us mountains of golden treasure to mine; it stays with us through every change in human fortune, never leaving us without considered instruction; it remains our dearest possession to the end of our lives. We are made to know wisdom: wisdom is not an instrument for living well; rather, the whole of life is the occasion for growth in wisdom.

And finally, we must speak of the sheer pleasure of learning in the school of God's universe. There is nothing so wonderful as to cross barriers of understanding that have so far been beyond our abilities. There is nothing so enlightening as to see a connection between events that before appeared unrelated. There is nothing so energizing as to notice the intricate combination of variables that bring about one thing as opposed to another. The learning of wisdom is not the means to an end. The proper approach is not to decide what we want in life — be it wealth, fame, ease of circumstances, or something else — and then go in search of whatever information is needed to acquire these things. The proper approach is just the opposite; the pursuit of wisdom is a divinely ordained charge in life governing the whole of existence. Wisdom is worth laying aside our wealth, our fame, or our ease of circumstances in order to find it. Why? Because it is above all things desirable. There is nothing in the universe that so satisfies the human person in the totality of experience than wisdom. Above all else, get wisdom.

Brothers and sisters, Jesus Christ is the wisdom of God. He was there with God before the world was made. All things were made by him, and his light shines brightly over the whole creation. Ultimately, all wisdom that we discover is the mirror of Christ's love. It is no wonder that it brings such deep delight, such serene contentment, such gratifying discernment. Wisdom leads to Christ; it is therefore the greatest voyage of all.

XIV

PSALM 72

Our psalm for today is one of several that modern scholars designate as "royal psalms." The royal psalms are not collected in any one part of the Psalter, but instead are scattered throughout. One of them, the second psalm, is placed in a prominent position, perhaps as a way of underscoring the important role these psalms play in the overall witness of the book of Psalms. Like the other royal psalms, Psalm 72 speaks of the rule of the righteous king. It is ascribed to David, and it clearly expresses the hope of a father for the well-being of his son, Solomon, to whom it is dedicated. Yet it was collected into the Psalter long after King David was dead; long after King Solomon was dead; indeed, long after the monarchy had ceased to exist as an institution in Israel. Why was it treasured in Israel's Scripture? Because faithful Israel heard in this intimate prayer of a father for his beloved son a true testimony to its own hope in the coming of God's Messiah. The rule of Solomon is a figure for the rule of God over the earth. Let us consider the promise that this psalm contains. Brothers and sisters, hear the Word of God.

The psalm begins with an appeal to God to exercise his supreme authority on behalf of the ruler, David, and to extend the gift of his faithfulness to the coming monarch, Solomon. David describes the kind of rule he wants for his son and commits into God's hand the activity of bringing it about. Let Solomon be a righteous king — that is, one who carries out his office with undying loyalty to the people for the common good — and let the power of his delivering hand embrace

165

those with limited resources. May peace in his kingdom be universal and comprehensive, and may it be founded upon the principles of justice. Let the aid of the king be focused especially upon the destitute and the children of those with limited means, and may it render null and void every attempt to contravene their welfare. May obedience be rendered to the king through every cycle of life and by every new generation of his people. Let the gracious rule of the king descend upon the earth like copious showers upon land rich in growth, like rains that irrigate the land from heaven above.

Jesus Christ is the one true fulfillment of the promise of the Old Testament. He is the sovereign ruler of all creation of whom this psalm ultimately speaks, whose dominion circumscribes the whole universe. He governs the totality of existence with absolute authority. Yet he is not a principle of "fate" that stands aloof from human life, nor an ironclad "necessity" that rules and overrules human desire. Christ the King of creation arranges the affairs of his earth for the sake of joy and growth in the lives of his disciples. If they have little, he makes sure that every single item they possess gives greater satisfaction and enrichment than all the riches ever stored up by humankind. Whatever the community of faith needs, he supplies in abundance, so that the life of the whole is constantly nourished. His special attention is devoted, not to the centers of churchly power and influence, but wherever his will is celebrated, no matter by how few, or how little esteemed they are. A new generation of his people arises, not where hype and public opinion predict, but wherever the young are cherished and raised in his honor. No circumstance will ever successfully contradict the effort to bring up a child in the nurture of the Lord, for Christ himself provides time and space for the love of children. The disciples of Christ do not worry for one instant about whether their decisions in life are applauded by others. They do what is right because it is commanded by Christ, and they teach their children to do the same in all circumstances. The blessing of Christ in the lives of his people is inexpressibly sweet, meeting needs scarcely discernible, giving cheer profoundly enlivening.

David continues his description of the rule he desires for his son. May the obedient in the land sprout during his rule. Let well-being for all last forever. May no obstruction set a limit to his dominion, which without boundaries includes the extreme limits of the world and all that it contains. Let even desert-dwellers serve him; and may those that rise up against him be destroyed. May surrounding kingdoms pay tribute to him, and even the distant coastlines render him homage; let remote and established realms offer their expensive bounty. Indeed, may every sovereign upon earth give obeisance to him and all nations of the world serve as his subjects. Again, it is worth reminding ourselves that this prayer was collected into Israel's Scripture long after the monarchy ceased to exist. The hope of Israel was not a glorification of the past or an enhanced elaboration of the present; the king whom they expected was the Messiah of God, whose kingdom has no end.

Jesus Christ is the Messiah of Israel, the Savior of all humankind. He is not limited to the East; he is Lord also in the West. He is not enclosed within the North; he rules also in the South. No earthly power can overshadow his sovereign purpose for good in the lives of his people. National boundaries do not define the limits of his will, which reaches to every corner of the globe. The customs of humankind do not undercut his commandments, which alone instruct all the earth in the knowledge of God. The social scale does not hinder his activity. He does what he pleases, standing above rich and poor alike, in the purity and impartiality of his truth. The flow of all human history is directed by him according to his hidden purpose. He never loses his focus upon those who trust in him; they soon discover that their efforts, however meager, come to maturity with explosive impact and that every dimension of their lives is rendered whole again by his compassionate care.

The tone of the prayer suddenly shifts, as David reflects upon a peculiar aspect of the hope he has for his son. It is one thing to govern all earthly powers with unlimited scope of authority. It is quite another to pay attention, not to those powers, but to the frail and the vulnerable. That is the secret of Solomon's kingdom. When the poor cry out for help, even though he is the exalted king, he does not turn a deaf ear; instead, he uses his royal prerogative to come to their rescue. He uses his regal splendor to uplift those who have reached the very end of the possibilities for human help. Their life does not come to an end when their resources are exhausted, because he makes their plight his own concern. Though they are without support of any kind, he makes sure that their lives are saved. When they experience cruelty or injury of any kind, he personally takes up their case; and any affliction that they must endure he treats with honor and passionate concern.

The presence of Christ shines the brightest in situations of human distress and need. Suffering does not close us off from Christ. The paradox is that the greatest benefits of his comfort are manifested most clearly where his love is needed the most. When those who honor the priorities for human existence that he himself has established must suffer consequences, they immediately realize that they are not alone in those consequences. Christ himself is there to show them each step along the way, to help them through every struggle, to build a future for them incomparably greater than every moment of the past. When obedience to Christ exacts a toll upon the availability of resources, the disciple quickly discovers that the economy of his love is richer than all wealth. When the decision of faith forces us into the unfamiliar and the untried, we suddenly come to understand who has been teaching us all along, and how precious are the lessons that he brings. Christ is nearest to those who suffer for his name; it has ever been so in the tender mercies of his kindness.

David concludes his prayer of hope for his son, the future king. May his life be long and filled with a fantastic abundance of acclaim. Let constant prayers be offered on his behalf, and may he receive the greetings of reverence at all times. May food be plentiful throughout his kingdom, and may every form of social life shine and sparkle. Let his name be established in perpetuity and his fame be spread abroad across the earth. May humankind seek blessing in his name and respond by offering him their praises. The psalm concludes with David's own benediction of worship to God, who rules Israel and who stands alone as the source of wondrous good in human life. Indeed, the wishes of a father for his son fold right into the recognition of the glorious domain of God over all things living and the exalted splendor of his eternal being.

Brothers and sisters, all that is good in your life has its source in the person of Christ. The loves you cherish are brought into your lives by him, who desires the expansion of your joy through affection for family and friends. The food that you eat, the clothes that you wear, the homes that you inhabit are given to you by him, who knows long before you do exactly what will please you the most. The good fun of human enjoyment is infused into your daily existence by him, who does not want you to spend a single day without constant reminder of his gracious will for your happiness. Why does he bring so much good into everything that you are and have? There is only one answer: it is because of his love. The love of Christ is, without comparison, the greatest good in all the earth. To know his love is the best destiny of all time.

XV

FROM THE BIRTH OF CHRIST

1. Matthew 1:18-25

We enter today upon the season of Advent, the time of the church year when we celebrate the mystery of the Incarnation. The great witness of Scripture is that God became a man in Jesus Christ, for the salvation of the earth. Witness to Christ is the true purpose of both Testaments of the Bible, and the church's one message to the world is the redeeming love of God through the gift of his Son. The birth stories are not meant to replace that grand confession; on the contrary, they everywhere presuppose it. They serve, rather, as a sign of the true meaning of what we believe. God became a human being; he entered into human space and time for the reconciliation of the world. There is no access to the divinity of Christ apart from his humanity. That is what the story of his birth compels us to consider, and to ponder, and to believe. Brothers and sisters, hear the Word of God.

What was it like, asks Matthew, when the Son of God was born into the world? Here is how it got started. His mother Mary was already engaged to Joseph; they were not married yet, and so they had never engaged in sexual intercourse. Everything is normal and routine, until something completely unexpected occurs. Mary becomes pregnant. Matthew tells us straight off that the child she is to bear has been conceived by the Holy Spirit. He doesn't go into any detail about what that means; he doesn't turn it into a philosophical lesson about supernatural happenings; he doesn't imply that something sexual is involved. He states straightforwardly that the birth of Christ is an absolute miracle. Mary is a virgin, yet she becomes pregnant through the Holy Spirit. His description of the event leaves open for the reader the same sense of astonishment with which it was greeted when it took place.

But Joseph has not yet been told what is going on. He sees only his beloved bride-to-be, upon whom the hopes of his whole life have been built, pregnant with a child that cannot possibly be his. We get a brief glimpse of the personality of Joseph as he reacts to the facts before him. He is a man of honor. Whatever overwhelming grief Mary may have caused him by her obvious adultery — for surely that is the only explanation for her condition — there is no point in making matters any worse than they already are. A woman in that day accused publicly of adultery would be forever disgraced. She would be an outcast from respectable company and branded for her whole life. However wounded his feelings may be, Joseph has no desire to put anyone through such a lifelong ordeal. So he decides to make a break with Mary in private, without any kind of scene.

But no sooner does he formulate his plan than it is rendered obsolete by startling new information. God sends an angel to tell Joseph the truth about Mary. His preconception about her condition is simply false. She has not been unfaithful; quite the opposite, her pregnancy has been brought about by God himself. There is no reason whatsoever why the marriage should not take place as planned. Even more, the angel fills Joseph in on the event to come. Her child will be a boy, whom Joseph is to name Jesus; he is the Messiah of Israel, whose role in life is to rescue God's people from their sins. At this point in the story, Matthew stands back for a moment as the narrator and addresses the reader directly; he wants to be sure that everyone understands what has just taken place. The birth of Christ to the virgin Mary is the direct fulfillment of the Old Testament promise concerning the entry of God into human history. He cites a specific verse from Isaiah to stress his point. Then Matthew completes his account. Joseph wakes up from the sleep that has brought him such good news and carries out to the letter what the angel has required of him. He goes through with the marriage to Mary, but waits to consummate their love until after she gives birth. He names the newborn child Jesus.

Christmas is first of all a time of year to reconsider the way we make our judgments about other people. Now, do not get me wrong; I firmly believe that our courts have a moral obligation to punish the guilty. No one is above the law, from the lowest to the highest in the land. I speak rather of the way we as Christians approach others in the give and take of everyday life. It is all too easy to take the observable facts at our disposal and reach negative conclusions that have the appearance of unassailable logic. Yet it may be that our conclusions are false and we have condemned the innocent. It could well be that we do not know what we think we know and that in fact we have missed the crucial truth that explains everything. I suggest a different approach. We must begin with the recognition that we cannot possibly know the story of another person's life. We can spin out our fantasies all day long, but the truth is that they are only the projections of our own imagination. They are not reality. We cannot approach other people as something known, to be evaluated; we must approach them as something unknown, as a mystery to be discovered. Evaluation is cold and calculating, and we do it badly. But discovery is provocative and alluring, and endlessly rewarding. Withhold judgment, and you will be surprised at the people you come to know for the first time.

Second, Christmas is a time to readjust the way we think about the future. Again, that is not to say that Christians should not be supremely responsible about the way they plan their lives. If times are lean, then it is up to us to make whatever changes must be made in order to accommodate a reduction in resources. Christian faith has nothing to do with a fatuous enthusiasm that ignores hard realities. Nevertheless, it is one thing to proceed with caution; it is quite another to draw conclusions from human history and to treat our conclusions as if they are prophetic predictions about tomorrow. The only way we could successfully make such predictions is if we ourselves stood outside the flow of time. And no one here does. Time is not an enemy to be defeated by human stratagem. The miracle of Christmas makes it clear that time is a friend of humanity, because God himself has sanctified it by his entrance into it. Time allows us not only to enjoy the end products of labor and desire but also to enjoy the countless stages of development that lead to them. Time creates opportunity for the human mind to explore the fantastic range of sound and color in the universe, with special emphasis upon details that can only be seen close-up. Time allows the human person to take in the full extent of God's gracious purpose for human welfare, which transcends every effort to state it in a systematic formula. Do not seek to conquer the future; submit to its pleasures, and you will not be disappointed.

Third, Christmas is a time to rekindle our sense of wonder about what is possible in God's universe. How many times in life have you given up on yourself, only to realize the next day that everything has altered overnight? How many times have you worried yourself sick about human circumstances, only to see every obstacle fall to the wayside and a well-marked path emerge from the dimness ahead? I do not refer to the power of positive thinking; positive thinking has nothing to do with it, for the human mind can change nothing about reality. The power of which I speak is not human at all, not in any sense of the word. It is God, who, from the very first moment of your existence to the present instant, has made the impossible occur in order to insure your vitality and contentment. Do not spend a single day this Advent season without reawakening your openness to what God has in store for you in the days and months ahead. He has long since earned your trust; do not withhold it, or you will miss the treasures of delight that it will bring.

And fourth, Christmas is a gift, of that there is no doubt; indeed, it is the true Gift behind every other gift. But the season of Christmas is also a time to cultivate again our appreciation of simple acts of obedience. God does not want us to save the world; but he does want us to make decisions in life that reflect his revealed will. God does not expect us to fight battles that are well beyond our means; but he does require a practical loyalty that affects the way we use the limited time and space he has provided for us. The real heroes in life are those who do on a daily basis the very things that they are assigned by God to carry out. Let us keep as our true ambition in life the image of a job well done, day in and day out, from one year to the next. All the glory of God is contained in the concrete act of obeying his command.

Brothers and sisters, the first week of Advent is a new beginning. The door is open. Do not hesitate; enter the door of life.

2. Matthew 2

Last week we began our series of Advent sermons by reflecting upon the annunciation to Joseph of the birth of the child Jesus. We observed Joseph's initial reaction to Mary's condition, a reaction that was overturned completely by his discovery of the true nature of what had occurred. We considered the need of every Christian to extend to others the benefit of the doubt in all circumstances, and the pleasant surprises in life that await all who live in patience. We also spoke of eager welcome toward the future; a welcome not confused with wishful thinking, but certainly not limited by human calculation. We noted the need to pursue even the smallest of obligations in life, for the majesty of God is more often than not located in the mundane and everyday. Today we turn to the well-known story of the Magi's visit; as with Christmas as a whole, the familiar retains the fullness of overflowing joy. Brothers and sisters, hear the Word of God.

The Gospel writer's account of the visit of the Magi presents powerful contrasts that highlight two different ways in which the good news of Christ's birth is received. The first contrast is that of place. The capital city of Jerusalem is the seat of religious authority, the cultural center of the nation, the location of a large population, all of whom are buzzing with terror and confusion about the visit of the three strangers from the East. The small town of Bethlehem is associated with a wonderful history, being the birthplace of King David. Nevertheless, it is a mere way-station on the main road from Jerusalem to Hebron in the south. Yet this small town becomes the focal-point of all creation; for here the Lord of the universe himself is born.

The second contrast presented in the story concerns the characters. On the one side is King Herod, the ultimate political demagogue; he is cruel, jealous, manipulative, dishonest, and ultimately lethal. On the other side are the three kings from the East, noble, wise, ardent, and relentlessly tenacious.

The final contrast is in the actions of the characters. Herod does everything he can to eliminate this perceived threat — badgering the religious leaders, using the wise men for information, plotting the death of the child. The wise men, however, travel a great distance to show honor to the new king. They have left the exotic lands of the ancient East and followed the star to a distant country; passing through the metropolitan city of Jerusalem, they finally arrive at the little town of Bethlehem. They are triumphant and joyful at what they find; for there in a house under the star that has shown them the way is a young woman with her child. He is the one they left home so long ago to find, and now they have found him. They kneel with reverence and bring out the costly gifts now known to every child: gold, frankincense, and myrrh. Through God's direct intervention, they escape Herod's trap and make their way home again.

Once a year, on Stewardship Sunday, it is the custom of this church to give every person an opportunity to make a pledge of financial contribution for the year to come. Whether or not you make a pledge is between you and God; how much you pledge is likewise a matter for your conscience alone. I would like to speak for a moment, however, about the motive for church giving. Numerous passages of the Bible address the question, but none is more eloquent or more powerful than the text before us. Why do we give? It is because of the passion of our devotion to Christ. We adore him who was born into this world on the first Christmas morning, who by his birth transformed every day of our existence into brightness and joy. We give out of love for Christ; not because we have to, not because it is expected or requested, but because to honor him with our whole being is our sole purpose in life.

As soon as the wise men depart, the story abruptly changes in tone. An angel warns Joseph in a dream to flee with his family down into Egypt, for Herod is about to do everything in his power to destroy the infant. They are to remain there until they are told to return. Joseph realizes that there is no time to lose, so he rises from bed, gathers his family, and leaves for Egypt in the dead of night. It is a scene of fear, with near destruction narrowly avoided, completely opposite to the previous scene of unbounded jubilation. The writer tells us that Joseph, Mary, and Jesus remain in Egypt until the death of Herod; he is so corrupt that there is no possibility of safe return to Israel as long as he is in power. Yet even the flight into Egypt is not a glitch in the divine plan; it is, on the contrary, the fulfillment of specific prophesy in the Old Testament. Herod finds out that his plot has failed and that the wise men have outsmarted him. His plan to murder Jesus quickly turns into a gruesome bloodbath of revenge and horror. Every child, two years old and under, in Bethlehem and the surrounding countryside is massacred in cold blood. Once again, the witness of the Old Testament has already prophesied the outbreak of grief and bitter agony that sweeps over the whole region.

The disciples of Jesus Christ are not somehow sealed off from difficult circumstances, nor even from great affliction. We share with all human beings periods in life when times of contentment and pleasure are suddenly interrupted, for who knows how long. We must all on occasion pass through trials of faith. Panic is our worst enemy, because it prompts us to make decisions that we later recognize as foolhardy. Denial is no better, because it blinds us to possibilities for recovery that lie before us. Withdrawal is the easy way out, yet the energy for living that fills our days will not ultimately be satisfied lying dormant. The key to confronting grave uncertainty or even momentous suffering is not to react to what we can only guess about tomorrow; instead, we must do today what we know is right and leave the future in God's hands. Concrete obedience is the right answer to even the most desperate threats to human happiness. Do not measure what you do today by its possible effect upon tomorrow; do today what you know you ought, and leave the rest up to God. He will accomplish his wondrous purpose, one way or another.

Herod dies; the reign of terror is ended. An angel appears again to Joseph down in Egypt and tells him that the time has come to return home. He is to gather up his beloved family and make the long trip back into the promised land. Joseph is informed that the ugly menace that threatened the child's life has now passed. The narrative records the response of Joseph with simple language; he carries out the angel's directive with total integrity. Yet the simplicity of the description carries for the reader an enormous affirmation of the faith of Joseph. Not so long ago he was forced to run for his life and to remove his precious family from imminent peril. Now he is being told to return to the country where the danger only recently loomed so large. Yet for Joseph the angel's declaration is enough: the one who sought the child's life is no longer alive. It is safe to return; and so Joseph takes those more dear to him than his own life back to the land of Israel. Even so, there is still trouble to avoid; he finds out that Herod's son, Archelaus, has inherited his father's throne. Can anything good be expected from the son of a mass murderer, who once targeted the life of his own boy? Joseph is understandably disturbed. But thankfully, a solution from God appears to him in a dream. He can return to the northern province of Galilee; it is part of the country of Israel, yet outside the specific jurisdiction of Archelaus. Joseph finds his way there and settles in the village of Nazareth, where he raises his family. Once again, the Gospel writer declares that already the Old Testament spoke of the future home of the Messiah, secured by the eternal plan of God.

Brothers and sisters, the Christmas season is a profound intersection of time and eternity. During this season we celebrate the mystery of the Incarnation. The eternal Son of God was born at a specific time and a definite place. The maker of Creation became a human being, with parents to watch over him, a whole life ahead of him, a mission to accomplish. On the one hand, his birth was a maze of astonishing events, some glorious, others horrendous. Yet on the other hand, the story of the birth of Christ is the unfolding of the promise of God, made explicit ages ago to the faithful of the land. The element of mystery in the Christmas season is for the vigorous encouragement of the Christian. If life at times appears to be a murky chaos, the Christmas message reminds us that in fact it is not: we can see only today, and no more; but there is One by whom tomorrow is not only known, but already determined. The eternity of God does not appear, as it were, unclothed; Jesus Christ is the eternity of God in human time, our time. Let us follow him into the future, for he has been there, and he knows the way.

3. Luke 2:1-20

We continue today our series of Advent sermons, based upon the story of the birth of Christ contained in the Gospels. Last week we followed the wise men from the East, through the dangerous encounter with Herod, and on to the small town of Bethlehem. There they found the newborn Christ, the object of all their seeking, and offered their gifts of love. We reflected upon that same love for Christ, which serves as the motive for giving in the church today. We then followed Joseph and his family as they fled for their lives down to Egypt to avoid the wrath of Herod. There they remained until the threat had passed. We spoke of the struggle of faith that confronts every Christian now and again, which can only be met with the response of daily obedience. We then saw Joseph bring his family back home to the promised land, where he brings up the child Jesus in the village of Nazareth. Despite the conflict of appearances, God's plan for our welfare is eternal and secure in every change of life. Today we observe the visit of the shepherds and the glorious joy of their discovery. Brothers and sisters, hear the Word of God.

Luke's Gospel makes it clear that not even the birth of Jesus takes place in a historical vacuum. The place of his birth, even the humble circumstances of his entry into the world, are all the product of historical forces affecting everyone. Rome is the world power in the West, and the Roman emperor decides to register all the subject peoples for the purposes of taxation. Luke records with some precision the exact sequence of events, since nothing like this had ever been tried. Every inhabitant must return with his family to his ancestral home, where he must officially record his name upon the census lists. So Joseph dutifully brings his fiancée down from Nazareth, to the town of Bethlehem, the place of birth of his great ancestor, King David. One can only imagine the turmoil of crowded roads, the snarl and tangle of a whole population on the move this way and that; but added to it all is the simple fact that Mary is pregnant and almost due. Yet travel they must, and quite a distance. But at the end of the journey they find that every room in town is already filled. The best Joseph can come up with is a little bit of space in an animal stall, and there Mary gives birth to the Savior of the world. She wraps the tiny baby up with strips of cloth to keep him warm and places him in a feeding-trough to sleep.

The church father Augustine was once asked to describe the Christian life, and he agreed to do so in three words: humility, humility, humility. The Christmas season is a time to shed every drop of pretension that has gathered upon us. If God has given us two or three tasks in life, let us not add a fourth and a fifth for good measure; instead, let us strive to do our two or three as best we possibly can, and trust in God to make our efforts count according to his good pleasure. When the mind strays to what we do not have, as if there lay the secret of happiness, let us quickly remind ourselves that we have been given the most astonishing gifts ever known to human life, every one of which overflows with unending springs of delight. If we are tempted to compare our circumstances with those of others, let us recognize that God has wondrously tailored our possessions and role in life to fit exactly what we need and to supply perfectly what we want out of life. Humility is not a lack of something; it is the way of God upon earth, and the surest road to every satisfaction.

As with Matthew's account of the visit of the Magi, so too Luke's portrayal of the birth of Jesus is full of contrast. For this modest and unpretentious scene suddenly shifts to one of brilliant splendor. In the fields around Bethlehem, there are shepherds living on the open land, where they take care of the flocks that provide their livelihood. It is the middle of the night, and no doubt the day has passed just like any other in a very routine existence. Without warning, without preparation, without any anticipation, their lives are changed forever. An angel appears to them, and the light of God's glory turns the darkness of night into unworldly day. They are stunned and overcome with terror. The angel soon reassures them: he has not come with a frightening message, but with incredible news of great joy for the whole of humankind. This very day, just over there in little Bethlehem, the Lord Christ has been born, the Redeemer of every creature. The angel gives them a clue to the enigma that he proclaims: they will find the little baby wrapped up tight and sleeping comfortably in the manger. Just as suddenly as the first angel appears, now he is joined by a countless throng of the hosts of God, all of whom sing their praises with exquisite beauty. "God dwells in heavenly glory," they sing, "and humankind is blessed by his kindness."

No thoughtful Christian can fail to be disturbed by the signs of dissension in the universal church. One faction battles with another faction for supremacy in a denomination; one denomination jockeys for position with another for leadership in the community of faith. It is well to be reminded in the Christmas season that we are not here for such purposes. We are here to preach and to believe the gospel, which contains the amazing message of salvation. The gospel is the peace of the church, gathering together into one a vast array of human personality, a fantastic range of talent and energy, a breathtaking assortment of contributions and legacies. The gospel is the hope of all the earth; it has guided generations in the past through the severest of afflictions, and it holds forth the promise of unchanging truth to every age to come. The gospel is the finest treasure of every individual Christian, the focus of all endeavors, the goal of all our loves, the repository of all our accomplishments in life. God became a man on that first Christian morning; the eternal God was born into this world there in that animal stall in Bethlehem. He did not stand back from human trouble; he did not hold us to account for the sins we have committed; he did not turn away from the hardships we face. He drew near, nearer than we are to ourselves, to bring comfort, guidance, and forgiveness. Jesus Christ is our Lord and Savior, and we belong to him alone.

Luke describes the reaction of the shepherds, once the angels fade away into the night sky. They turn to one another and agree with enthusiasm: "Let's go to Bethlehem and see what this is all about. God hasn't told us all these things for nothing; let's drop everything and head into town and see with our own eyes what has been described to us." They lose no time, and soon they arrive at the very place where Joseph and Mary have ended up after their long journey. The shepherds see precisely what they had hoped: the little baby lying in a manger. Now they know it is all true. They begin to tell everyone who will listen just what they have seen and what they have been told concerning the meaning of this child's birth for all humanity. Here is another of Luke's contrasts, for these are simple shepherds speaking earnestly of God's gracious plan for the entire creation. Those who hear them are startled by their testimony. But Mary's reaction is different; she listens carefully to what they say and stores it away in her memory as something precious and lifelong. The shepherds return to the fields, giving joyous thanks to God for directing them to the child and for the unspeakable grandeur of what they found. It is the best night of life, the night that turns all of life into day.

To do God's will with eagerness is what makes life a profound pleasure and an enduring miracle. There is nothing so serene as priorities faithfully aligned. There is nothing so exhilarating as the endeavor to carry out the divine imperative, with the assurance of such wondrous results in the end. There is nothing so enlivening as to act upon the divine promise, which has never once failed any who rely upon it. Why is God's will the source of such total enrichment for every facet of human experience? The commandments of God are not a list of onerous obligations, to be juggled and shuffled until all sense of perspective is lost. The commandments of God all lead to Jesus Christ. We obey them, because we know that Christ accompanies us on the path that they mark out. We give our all, because ultimately every act of obedience is a tribute to Christ's love. We forever remember to do them, because behind them all stands the person of Christ, urging us on to the triumph of life in his service. Christmas joy is the divine gift that comes with the search for fresh obedience to Christ. Seek him, and you shall have it.

Brothers and sisters, the wise men have brought their gifts; the shepherds have brought their rejoicing. As we draw nearer to Christmas, we draw nearer to the Savior of all humankind, whom to find is life forevermore. Glory to God in the highest. Peace on earth, good will to all.